Through Slanted Windows

A Journey into Radio

BY

DAVE ARCHARD

∞ INFINITY
PUBLISHING

All rights reserved. No part of this book shall be reproduced or transmitted in any form or by any means, electronic, mechanical, magnetic, photographic including photocopying, recording or by any information storage and retrieval system, without prior written permission of the publisher. No patent liability is assumed with respect to the use of the information contained herein. Although every precaution has been taken in the preparation of this book, the publisher and author assume no responsibility for errors or omissions. Neither is any liability assumed for damages resulting from the use of the information contained herein.

Copyright © 2012 by Dave Archard

ISBN 978-0-7414-7607-4 Paperback
ISBN 978-0-7414-7608-1 eBook

Printed in the United States of America

Published January 2013

∞

INFINITY PUBLISHING
1094 New DeHaven Street, Suite 100
West Conshohocken, PA 19428-2713
Toll-free (877) BUY BOOK
Local Phone (610) 941-9999
Fax (610) 941-9959
Info@buybooksontheweb.com
www.buybooksontheweb.com

To my wife for putting up with
a radio man all these years.

CONTENTS

The Gift 1
Mom, Dad And Tom 7
My Hometown 10
Listening With Mom 15
WWII 18
The Chubby Radio 23
A Boy's Life 27
Radio All Week Long 33
It's Elementary 40
The Book 46
First Try 49
The Tour 56
My Loss 65
Ben Franklin 71
Jerry And Uncle Miltie 75
Dad's City 79
Airwaves At Night 84
Tom 91
Leaving With A Bang 94
Senior Academe 97
Wally And Mary 101
Halsey And The Silver Machine 107

Class Act	111
Night Calls	115
The Ham Is Done	125
High Times	130
Working Toward A Goal	138
The Great Atlantic And Pacific Tea Company	142
Mixing Radio With Work	148
Factory Facts	153
Jazzbo, Moondog And Johnny	156
Riding The Rails	166
The ABC Of Radio And Television	173
Block And Ernie	179
Broadcasting 101	186
Sneaking In On Arthur	195
One Night In Clifton	200
Getting The Gig	206
Heading Out To Radioland	212
Hello Florence And Myrtle	218
Meet And Greet	221
Learning The Ropes	225
First Time	231
Reality Of The Job	239
My Big Error	243
Morning Glory	252
Half The Dream	259
Coda	268

THE GIFT

Standing on the sandlot, I cringed and held out my glove whenever the ball bounced my way. I couldn't catch or throw worth a darn, so when teams were chosen, I was picked last and banished to the weeds of right field.

In 1945, most nine-year-old boys in Ridgewood, New Jersey, dreamed of playing baseball before crowds in Yankee Stadium, but I longed to be at a microphone in a studio at NBC and talk to millions of people across the country. I wanted to be on the radio.

After a Sunday broadcast by Edgar Bergen and Charlie McCarthy, I looked forward to classmates gathered around me the on the schoolyard the next morning. "Do Mortimer Snerd again," one of them would say. I'd stick out my upper teeth to make me sound like the character on the program and repeat one of his lines with the appropriate timing.

"Yep, yep, that's. . . the way I heard it!"

The kids laughed and clapped. A tingling sensation went through me and I grinned from ear to ear. The ham was beginning to cook.

Miss May, the fourth-grade teacher at Kenilworth Elementary, overheard my performance. "David, you have the gift of mimicry," she said. I didn't know what the word meant, so I looked it up in the heavy dictionary in the school library. As I read the definition, a light came on in my head. *Whaddaya know! I can do something better than muffing fly balls in right field!*

* * *

I kept a two-wheel Schwinn in the garage and had a stash of comic books under my bed, but the big Zenith radio in the living room became the touchstone of my young life. Sliding off my chair after dinner in the kitchen, I scampered across the hall to my bedroom. After I peeled off my school clothes, I left them in a pile on the floor and grabbed my pajamas. In my rush to put them on, I pulled the top on inside out and ran into the living room.

I stood at a tall brown cabinet with four squat legs and a round dial the size of a saucer opposite my face. When I snapped a knob shaped like a chocolate drop, the dial lit up and glowed yellow revealing a smattering of numbers from 540 to 1600. I turned the dial to 710 and static crackled behind the fuzzy fabric as WOR began to fade in from New York. I bounced in anticipation.

"Dave? The dishes," my mother called from the kitchen. *Oh, phooey.* I ran in to where Mom had plates from dinner dripping water in a rack. Drying each with a quick swipe of a towel, I strained to hear the radio in the next room. Only the faint sound of the Three Suns organ, accordion and guitar came through the wall.

Finishing the chore, I threw the towel under the sink, ran back to the living room and assumed my position at the big radio as Gabriel Heatter's voice came on.

"Ah, there's good news tonight," he said. *Darn, it's the commentator man.* Disappointed, I lay on the rug and waited until something more exciting came on.

My father sat in an overstuffed chair under a floor lamp. Using the corner of a book of matches, he cleaned remnants of dinner from between his teeth, gave *The New York Journal American* a few shakes and began to read. The commentator droned on and if he mentioned the war or something called "the economy," Dad lowered the paper to listen.

Having no interest in what the man said, I pulled my mother's *Radio Mirror* from the magazine rack and thumbed through the pages. Photos showed people at microphones in front of slanted windows and I imagined myself standing with them.

Mom came in from the kitchen, sat on the davenport and shared the light of the floor lamp to mend socks. My older brother, Tom, stretched out beside me and reached over and punched me on my arm for no reason. When Mr. Heatter stopped talking, I pushed the magazine away.

Because I knew when all the shows came on and at what spot on the dial, my parents allowed me to change stations. As I got up, my brother grabbed the leg of my pajama bottom and yanked.

"Quit it!" I yelled.

My father grunted from behind his newspaper. "Let him go, Tom," he said.

I pulled up my pajamas, moved to the big radio with the measured steps of a king approaching his throne and sang: "Dot ti-ti daaa."

"Oh, brother," Tom muttered. "Just do it."

Using thumb and forefinger, I turned the station knob like a safe cracker finessing a combination lock, moving the dial's thin needle to set it precisely on 660. Doing an about-face like a soldier on guard duty, I marched to my place on the rug and lay down again.

Dad laughed as three funnymen told jokes in rapid succession on *Can You Top This?* Next, an audience on *The Pepsodent Show* howled at something Bob Hope said that got past the censor: "If women's skirts get any shorter, they'll have two more cheeks to powder." I didn't understand the remark and looked up at Mom. She shook her head.

Later, when I turned the dial to 880 for the *First Nighter* program, the sound of New York traffic put me right in a taxi as I rode with the host of the program. At the curb outside the Little Theater off Times Square, an usher opened the door.

"Your seats are waiting, Mr. First Nighter."

I imagined myself walking with him through a crowd buzzing in the lobby. Settled in our seats, he told about the play I was going to see in my mind's eye. Then a call went out.

"Curtain. First curtain."

Mr. First Nighter lowered his voice.

"The house lights have dimmed, and the curtain is about to up on tonight's production of *Something in the Air* starring Olan Soule and Barbara Luddy."

Putting my head down, I let the radio sweep me away to meet sophisticated people in glamorous settings until I heard Mom's voice: "Time for bed, Dave." I wanted to stay in front of the big radio, but got up and stumbled half awake across the hall.

* * *

Two beds and a dresser were crammed in the small room I shared with my brother. Under the lone window, an iron radiator hissed steam and dripped water in the winter. A black shade got pulled down for air raid drills at night and to darken the room during the day the time I had the measles. In the summer, Mom left open the top half of a Dutch door facing the backyard to let in a breeze and the sound of crickets.

Before drifting off to sleep, I could hear the radio in the living room across the hall. On Sunday night, I pictured the characters who kibitzed with Fred Allen when he knocked on their doors in *Allen's Alley*. The following morning, I imitated their voices and dialects on the schoolyard.

First, Titus Moody, the old man from New England: "Howdy, bub, ahhh."

Next, Ajax Cassidy, the Irishman: "Ooo, it's a good day to ya, lad."

Then Senator Claghorn, the bombastic politician: "I'm proud to be – I say, I'm proud to be from the South, son."

Last, Mrs. Nussbaum, the Jewish lady from Brooklyn: "You were expecting maybe Weinstein Churchill?"

When classmates laughed, the funny sensation went through me again. *How great it'll be when my voice goes out on the air and people laugh from coast to coast. Then I'll feel the tingling all the time.*

* * *

Sundays were like Christmas to me then. I jumped out of bed and rushed into the living room. The excitement was just outside the front door. Opening it, I lifted the thick *New York Herald Tribune* off the stoop. Laying the newspaper on the rug in the living room, I knelt and shuffled through the sections. The *Herald Tribune* had no comics, but another treat was buried in the folds, and I hurried to find it.

On the front of the first section was a bold headline about the war. A section with business news followed, then sports, glossy *This Week* magazine, and the classified ads for jobs and homes. My father would read the paper after church, so I was careful not to tear anything. At last, my fingers touched a small stapled booklet. Pulling it out, I waved it in the air. *Got it!*

Every Sunday, the black and white *Radio Guide* in the *Herald Tribune* had a photo of a personality on the cover. The first time I discovered it, I was delighted to see an announcer I'd heard so often. Ben Grauer's face was pressed against a microphone with letters N B C across the top.

The following week, I devoured an article about an actress in a daytime drama, but didn't understand how she got on the radio by working in something called "the Broadway theater."

Each issue had a page for each day of the week with columns of programs for eight New York stations. Running my finger down the tight grids, I squinted at the titles in small type to make sure my favorite shows would be on. At the top of each column next to the stations' call letters were frequency numbers, but I knew by heart where they were on the dial. Putting the booklet against my chest, I bragged to my brother.

"I can tell you all the stations without looking, even the ones with baseball and the one at the end that plays symphonies."

Although my father came home in the evening with the *Journal American* tucked under his arm, I was happy he had the *Herald Tribune* delivered to the house on Sunday.

Without uttering a word, I poured over every story and photo in that wonderful little booklet. Mom wondered why I was so quiet. "Is Dave all right?" she'd ask Dad.

MOM, DAD AND TOM

At dinner one evening, I asked my parents about our family roots. My father liked to tell stories with great exaggeration, so what he related was more than I wanted to hear.

"An Archard came over with William the Conqueror when the Normans invaded Saxony," he claimed. "Back in France, there was always an Archard hanging from a tree for stealing a horse or a basket of apples." I shuddered imagining the body of an ancestor twisting in the wind.

My father, Herb Archard, grew up in the early 1900s in a tough German neighborhood of New York City. His mother kept his hair cut like a Dutch boy.

"Bangs on my forehead and hair over my ears made me stick up for myself with my fists when I was teased on the street," he said.

In 1920, Dad was in his last year of high school. He was a whiz at math and would graduate second in his class, but his mother took him out of school and got him a job as a bookkeeper.

"Parents did that back then, so children could bring money into the household instead of wasting time in school," he explained. *How cruel*, I thought.

By the forties, Dad was zone business manager for the Oldsmobile division of General Motors. He made sure dealerships in northern New Jersey, Connecticut and Long Island kept accounting books to prosper the GM way. At the first Christmas in the new house, I helped Mom bring in wicker baskets of fruit, meat and liquor that arrived at the door from appreciative dealers.

My father was six feet tall, had a bald head, a beer belly and flat feet that required him to slip metal arches in his shoes. He didn't look tough on the outside, but his personality had been shaped by his harsh upbringing, and he was often gruff with my brother and me. I overheard him talk once to Mr. Doscher, our next door neighbor: "Glen, I wouldn't sell my boys for a million bucks, but I wouldn't give you a plug nickel for another." Although Mom did the spanking, a scowl from Dad was enough to make me obey.

My mother, Dorothy, was from the affluent Davidson family of Darien, Connecticut. Slender with brown hair and doe eyes, Mom did modeling as a teenager for a department store in Stamford. In her twenties, her good looks landed her the lead in a silent movie shot by an amateur filmmaker. With a wonderful singing voice, she sang to the radio in the kitchen and with Dad in the car. Whenever I asked her a silly question, she'd make a funny face that never failed to make me laugh.

I had to go to school the day Mom planned to take the train to visit her mother in Montclair, New Jersey. Going out the door, I planted a thought in her ear: "Well, you know, Grandma Davidson is getting older. I might not get to see her for very long,"

Later that morning, my soft-hearted mother surprised me by showing up outside my classroom. The office secretary told Miss May that I could be dismissed for the day.

Walking hand-in-hand with Mom, I left the building and we headed for the train station.

Although Mom was raised in a wealthy family, I never heard her complain about tending to a husband and two sons in a middle-class home. Her one extravagance was sending the laundry out to Bon Ton Cleaners. My friends' homes had wringer washing machines in the basement. Ours didn't.

I never appreciated all my mother did for me. With youthful abandon, I accepted her love and thought nothing of it. I had no idea what would happen later.

My brother had a sharp nose and chin for a kid of fourteen. Tom would frown and assume a superior attitude when I was around. "Don't lay your bike down like that. You'll ruin the handle bars," he'd say. Because he was a big ninth grader at Benjamin Franklin Junior High in 1945 while I was a mere fourth grader in Kenilworth Elementary, we didn't have the same friends, but we played together often and quarreled and fought. As much as I disliked the way my big brother bossed me around at times, I wanted to do everything he did. After watching Tom bounce his bicycle off a plywood ramp in the driveway or skip flat stones across the brook at the end of the street, I had to imitate him and do the same.

MY HOMETOWN

Our family moved in to our home in Ridgewood, New Jersey, in 1941, a month before the attack on Pearl Harbor. The two-bedroom one-bath house on Albert Place sat with others in a subdivision carved out of the woods on the east side of town. While the house was being built, we lived in a rental home in Mamaroneck, New York and drove over on weekends to check the progress. Mom and Dad became excited when they saw pipes and frames rising from the cinder block foundation.

Other cracker box houses on the block were the homes of kids – Terry Corbin, Fritz Williams, Raymond Shanahan and on the next street over, Frankie Ketz. As World War II raged, we dug foxholes in the vacant lot at the end of the street and kept Nazis at bay with fake guns of plastic and wood.

The developers of the subdivision lived in the neighborhood themselves. Joe Tognolli took a two-story house at the end of Albert Place and his brother Phil built a low rambling one called a "ranch" on a choice lot with slender birch trees. After a heavy rain, water seeped through the foundation of the basement in our home. I thought it was funny to see bits of wood floating around like little boats in

Dad's workshop as my father grumbled and swore as he waded around, trying to rescue what he could. After renting a gasoline-powered pump to get the water out, he made sure the Tognolli brothers heard from him, but they never came and sealed the basement.

The first time a house payment was due on our new home, I heard my father gripe to my mother about the mortgage: "A total of five thousand dollars over the next thirty years. Christ."

* * *

Weekends and in the summer, I didn't tell my mother where I was headed or what I was going to do. I was out the door and gone after breakfast. Mom was trusting and prayerful and when I came home at lunch or dinner with all my limbs, she was thankful.

Frankie Ketz and I wanted to explore more of our hometown than the neighborhoods between our homes and school. On a bright Saturday morning, we climbed on our bikes and ventured deeper into the wilds of Ridgewood.

We rode past the older homes of working folks on the east side and rushed by Kenilworth Elementary. *What else is beyond the stone building with teachers who smelled of flowery perfume?* Beyond the school, we entered downtown bustling with traffic and shoppers.

At the Warner Theater, I put on the brakes and looked up. On a chrome marquee wrapping around the front, words heralded a movie starring someone with the odd name Humphrey Bogart, but I knew Roy Rogers and Gene Autry would be found inside. A woman in a small glass booth underneath the marquee smiled as Frankie and I swung on our bikes and continued our exploration. Further up the street, I saw a train station and pumped harder on the pedals.

Among the trees of Bergen County, the Village of Ridgewood was split in two by the Erie Railroad. A set of four shiny tracks descended from Ho Ho Kus to the north and disappeared down the line to Glen Rock. Trains came in and stopped on the outside rails or whizzed through on the inside ones without slowing down. Wind from the morning express blew my hair back as it flashed by bound for Chicago.

Trains letting passengers on and off at the station were called "locals." They were pulled by honest-to-goodness steam locomotives, big iron work horses that screeched and hissed as they glided in to a platform. Black smoke lingered in the air after they huffed and puffed and chugged away. At night, wailing whistles of freight trains reached across town to my bedroom.

Two tunnels, one for vehicles and a narrow one for pedestrians, went under the four sets of tracks. Openings at the ends of the narrow one had steps down one side for walkers and a long sloping ramp down the other for bicycle riders and moms with baby carriages. Frankie and I stood at the top of a ramp until puffs of smoke announced a local coming in from Glen Rock. As it got closer, we dove with our bikes into the tunnel.

The air underneath the tracks smelled musty and felt cool. The cement floor was spotted with puddles, peeling plaster hung from the ceiling and bare light bulbs glared behind metal grates. *This is Dracula's castle!* When tons of iron and steel from the local rumbled over our heads, I shivered and yelled and the sound of my voice bounced off the walls.

After walking our bikes up the ramp on the west side, we settled on the seats and traveled along streets that were wider and smoother than the bumpy ones back in our neighborhood. Passing lush green lawns sloping up to a row of mansions, I called back to Frankie: "This is where my father says the rich people live." Stopping by a home with white pillars in front, I stared at a long black car at the top of a circular driveway and imagined a chauffer sitting inside, ready to drive a family to a show or fancy restaurant. At a stately building ringed by manicured shrubbery, gold letters above the double doors spelled "Ridgewood Women's Club." *I wonder what women do inside. Maybe Mom can join and I'll find out.* Turning our bikes around, we headed back to the train station.

Emerging from the tunnel, we weaved down a street along the railroad tracks. A block beyond the A&P, we stopped at a three-story brick apartment house. Staring at dark-skinned boys and girls playing kick the can and hop scotch on the sidewalk, I whispered to Frankie: "Those are the Negro kids who go to Union Street School." I heard neighbors on our block talk to my parents in derogatory terms about the people who lived in the apartments. One woman in the neighborhood yelled at us kids for putting our mouths under the water tap by her kitchen door to take a drink, because she said Negro men did the same when they came around every week to pick up the garbage. I felt uneasy about joining the fun at the apartment house, so Frankie and I pushed off again on our bikes and pedaled further east, anxious for the lunches our moms had waiting at home.

* * *

My brother surprised me one day by talking in his "big brother" voice.

"Jewish people can't buy homes in Ridgewood. I heard Dad tell Mr. Baird across the street that if a Jewish couple meets with a real estate agent, he shuffles through his listings and says he has nothing to show them. Jews can run stores here, but they have to be out of town by sundown."

That didn't seem right. Jerry Goodman was in the same Cub Scout pack as I was and I thought he was an okay kid, but then he lived over the line in Glen Rock. I don't know if being a "restricted town" is what attracted my father to move to Ridgewood. I never asked him.

The Village of Ridgewood, New Jersey, was typical of towns in 1945 with its share of closet drinking, illicit affairs and racial and religious bigotry. As an innocent kid of nine, though, I thought it was a wonderful place to ride a bicycle.

LISTENING WITH MOM

I faked an illness one cold morning because I hadn't written a book report for school. Coming in the kitchen, I coughed and made my voice sound raspy.

"I don't feel so good."

My father looked at me suspiciously over his cup of coffee. Mom put her hand on my forehead and a thermometer under my tongue. Luckily, it came out a little high.

"All right, get back in bed," she said. I darted out of the kitchen. "But you're to stay there and there'll be no playing in the house."

Lining up a regiment of lead soldiers on my bedspread, I nosedived at them with a model of a P-40 Mustang. After a few strafes with the plane, I brought down the collection of Tootsie Toys from the shelf above my pillow. Placed on the lumps of the spread, the little metal cars just sat there. Getting out of bed, I whipped them across the floor on their little rubber tires. When they crashed into the baseboard, I scrambled back in bed in case Mom might hear them and look in my room.

Bored, I leaned over and grabbed comic books from under the bed. Flipping through them, I discarded each one -

The Green Lantern, Captain America and *Archie Andrews. Which ones haven't I read a hundred times?*

After Dad left for work and Tom for school, I heard Mom switch stations on the table model radio by the toaster in the kitchen. The dark brown plastic casing of the receiver had rounded corners, a crescent-shaped dial, and slots for the speaker on the front. They were separated by the on-off knob and station knob stacked one on the other. When the radio was snapped on, tubes inside heated up and warmed the casing. From my bed, I was going to hear what she listened to during the day.

A band, singers and an Aunt Fanny marched around a breakfast table in Chicago. Don McNeill let the audience say a silent prayer "each in his own way."

Next, Arthur Godfrey and his little Godfreys sang and joked around. The show was broken into six quarter-hour segments for a marathon ninety minutes. At the end of every segment, the band's trombone player slid into the first note of Godfrey's theme song. I imitated it and sang.

"Burrr-rup… 'Seems Like Old Times.'"

The daily dramas took over. Mom's *Radio Mirror* said they were called "soap operas" because the sponsors were selling laundry detergent. They all sounded the same to me. While an organ played, a sincere announcer reminded my mother what she had heard the day before, then men and women came on to complain about love and sickness until the organ ended with a flourish and Mom was told to "tune in again tomorrow."

At noon, I padded to the kitchen in slippers for a bowl of Campbell's chicken noodle Mom heated from a can. Looking at the counter where the radio sat, I laughed.

Our big family cat was lying on top of the set, enjoying the warmth from the tubes. His body completely hid it as *The Romance of Helen Trent* came out of his fur.

After I slurped the soup, Mom shooed the cat off the radio to tune from CBS to NBC and I retreated to my bedroom. A long parade of soap operas followed. There was *Portia Faces Life* and *Life Can Be Beautiful*, *Young Widder Brown* and *Young Doctor Malone*, *Backstage Wife* and *John's Other Wife*. Mom dialed back and forth for three hours to hear her favorites.

Moving through the house to dust, she turned on the big radio in the cabinet and the programs came booming into the sanctity of my room. I closed the door hoping to block the agony and misery. With pad and pencil, I struggled to write my book report, but it was hard to concentrate with all that was going on outside my door. I should have done this last night, I thought with regret.

When the adventure serials came on at five, I recovered from my supposed illness and went to the living room to listen. By dinner time, I was my old self again.

"Nine o'clock fever this morning," my father called it when he got home.

I went to school the next day.

WWII

A shrill blast from a policeman's whistle startled me one night. Mr. Eagleson, the air raid warden on Albert Place, was outside our house during a blackout drill.

"Douse that light!" he yelled. My parents hadn't pulled down a black window shade far enough to help darken the neighborhood from possible enemy bombers.

The war continued in 1945. The Army pushed towards Germany, the Marines moved closer to Japan and Frankie Ketz and I stood guard from our foxholes in the subdivision.

I sang along to the radio when the song "Praise the Lord and Pass the Ammunition" came on and dutifully bought little red stamps at school to raise money for guns and bombs. Mom let me bust the orange tablet in a plastic bag of oleomargarine and knead the coloring through the white glop to make it look like butter. While playing guns with the kids in the neighborhood, I'd hear a deep growl under my plastic army helmet that meant the wind tunnel at West Caldwell had been cranked up to test a fighter plane.

One Sunday, Uncle Joe visited with Aunt Adeline from Union City, New Jersey, and he let me sit behind the wheel of his Lincoln Zephyr. He had pasted a label with the number 35 on the dashboard above the speedometer.

"What's that?" I asked.

"That reminds me to drive under thirty-five miles an hour to save gasoline for planes and ships," he said.

* * *

My father was let go from Oldsmobile when the company switched over to build tanks. He was hired by American Cyanimide, a chemical company headquartered in New York, but no company car was in the deal like he had with Oldsmobile. He joined countless men and a few women in Ridgewood, and became a commuter.

Mornings after seven, he put the steel supports in his shoes and walked up Albert Place to catch the bus to the Erie station downtown. He boarded a train to Jersey City where a shiny rail car took him under the Hudson River in a "tube" to the tip of Manhattan. He caught a subway uptown and arrived at his office in Rockefeller Center by nine. To get home at five o'clock quitting time, Dad repeated the route in reverse. We didn't eat dinner much before seven.

Once Dad took our family on the bus, train, tube and subway journey to visit his office. How thrilling it was when I saw the chemical company was in the same building as Radio City with people gathered at microphones in studios with slanted windows.

I felt like a celebrity entering the RCA Building under the gray and chrome overhang with red neon letters that spelled "NBC STUDIOS." As we rushed past the carpeted stairs leading to the network, I stopped and looked up.

"That's where I wanna go," I said, but Mom pulled me toward the elevators.

Disappointed, I hung my head as I followed the family, and we rode high above the magical floors of the National Broadcasting Company. *Maybe some other time.*

* * *

Seated with my parents at the Warner Theater one night in 1945, I watched a stark newsreel. In a city destroyed by bombs in Europe, a boy and girl pushed a baby carriage through the rubble with their belongings piled high. I hadn't realized how fortunate I was to lie in bed in a safe home and listen to the radio while kids on the other side of the world were experiencing the horrors of war.

* * *

In August, my brother and I would play ball in the street before the sun went down. Two girls, Jean and Edna, came out of their houses often to join us followed by an only child rich kid. Chubby and slow on his feet, Chester Greenleaf owned the newest baseball, bat and glove, so we let him play. It was more fun, though, to throw a worn tennis ball in the air and smack it with the cut-off handle of a broom. We'd chase the ball over the neighbors' lawns and the batter had to stop it when it was thrown back or the ball would roll all the way down to the end of Albert Place.

After one sweaty game ended and the mosquitoes began to bite, Chester motioned us into his garage.

"Look at this, you guys," he said holding out a stick of railroad dynamite. His father was an executive with the Erie Railroad. "When the war's over, my dad's gonna set this off!"

We could hardly wait.

The day Japan surrendered, my mother told Tom and me to be cleaned up before Dad got home.

"We're going to church," she said.

"But the dynamite!" I whined.

"Yeah, Mr. Greenleaf's going to light it when it gets dark," Tom said.

Mom shot us "the look" and our family went to a prayer service at First Presbyterian Church that evening. The next day, Chester showed us the hole in the street where the dynamite was ignited. Tom and I looked at each other and shook our heads at the blast we missed.

* * *

When the war ended, Oldsmobile stopped making tanks and began making cars again, so Dad went to the General Motors Building to get his job back. When he arrived home, I heard him talking to my mother.

"Now the war's over, GM isn't hiring anyone over thirty-five. Ridiculous."

My father was 43, and I worried. *What if he's fired from the chemical company? What if there's nothing to eat, and we lose our home? Will I be out on the street pulling our belongings in my wagon like the kids in the newsreel?*

"Hell, I went uptown to Packard," Dad continued. "They hired me right away and I'm getting a company car next week." *Wow, a car. A Packard!*

* * *

The black cradle phone on the kitchen counter rang one morning and Mom called out. "It's for you, Dave."

Joe Rector, a kid from the neighborhood over the hill on Laurel Road, was on the line.

"My dad's coming home!" he yelled.

His father, Joseph Rector, Sr., enlisted in the army as a youth, worked his way up in rank and was a lieutenant colonel by the time the war broke out. He landed in North Africa to fight the Nazi Panzer Division in the desert. Because Joe was without a dad during the war, his mother took me aside one day.

"Would you teach Joe how to ride a two-wheeler?" she asked quietly. "Okay," I whispered, feeling special that I was aiding the war effort.

The night the lieutenant colonel returned home, jubilant neighbors came out from homes for blocks around and gathered in front of the Rectors' house. Two men on ladders had strung a line of light bulbs across the street. A photographer from the *Ridgewood Herald News* showed up with a flash camera. Someone blew notes on a bugle.

I was packed in the crowd with my brother, standing on tiptoe to see. Up on their front porch, Joe, his mother and sister craned their necks as an olive-drab sedan moved slowly through the crowd. It stopped and a tall, tanned man got out of the back. He wore a brown uniform and a cap with a shiny black bill, his chest covered with ribbons and medals. The crowd let out a tremendous roar.

For the east side of Ridgewood, New Jersey, the war was finally over.

THE CHUBBY RADIO

Dad was handy with tools, so he built a bedroom for my brother and me in the attic of the house. Our two beds fit snuggly under the eaves of the roof, and I could look over the neighbor's roof from the window and see the woods going down to the brook at the end of the street.

To my delight, my mother placed a chubby little plug-in radio on the shelf above my pillow. When Tom and I moved into the new bedroom, she got an extra room downstairs and I got the freedom to listen to whatever I wanted whenever I wanted upstairs.

First chance I got, I lay in my bed and placed the radio on my stomach. It had a brown plastic casing like the set in the kitchen, only smaller. I snapped the knob on the left and the radio came alive in my hand. A crackling noise started behind the speaker slots on the front.

Turning the radio around, I looked through a hole in the stiff cardboard backing. Tiny red and yellow flames flickered in glass tubes, and as they warmed the Bakelite in the casing, the radio gave off a sweet aroma.

The knob on the right was the magical one. My parents let me tune to four frequencies on the big radio in the living room, 710 and 770 for adventure serials in the afternoon and

660 and 880 for comedies and dramas in the evening. *How many other stations can I find now?* Twisting the knob all the way to the left, I made the thin needle stop at 54.

Twisting it the other way, the needle moved and a station came in. The announcer talked about the Giants at their spring training camp in Florida. After he gave the call letters, WMCA, I started the needle again.

A soap opera was on at WEAF. *I know that station. It has all the great NBC programs at night.* I laughed at the main character's name, "Stella Dallas." Twisting the dial, I landed on WOR just as an announcer gave the time.

"It's 1:45, Bulova Watch time. B-u-l-o-v-a. Bulova!" I tried to spell the name out loud as fast as the announcer did, but couldn't.

Next came WJZ with a man and woman talking about a Broadway show they saw the night before. It didn't interest me, so I moved to the needle again. At the following station, a woman talked to an author about a book he wrote. I waited patiently until the station was identified as WNYC. An announcer said it was owned by the City of New York.

Another twist and another soap opera started from CBS on WABC. *How funny the CBS station has the call letters WABC.* I heard a bobwhite whistle twice, and a woman sang like the bird: "Rin-so White! Rin-so White!"

Smack in the middle of the dial, a station came through so loud I had to turn down the volume. An announcer said it was WPAT in Paterson, New Jersey. *Hey, that's not too far from Ridgewood.* I put the fact away in my head.

The needle moved and caught WAAT in Newark. Peppy fiddles and sliding guitars made me linger at the music before the announcer on *Hometown Frolics* said it was "country and western." *The singers sure sound different than the way people talk in New Jersey.*

WINS was next followed behind by WHN. Both played records and the announcers talked about Yankee and Dodger spring training in Florida.

After listening to a Dinah Shore record finish on WNEW, I inched the needle along as the dial grew tight with signals. A man babbled in a strange language and then another calling himself a "reverend" came through. He thundered about hell and damnation from his "pillar of fire." Frightened by what he said, I didn't linger to hear the call letters.

The needle slid past a man talking in a foreign language. To a kid of nine, it sounded like jabbering to me. The needle came to rest on WQXR. I listened for a moment to a symphony orchestra, but the violins made me sleepy. Finally, the needle stopped at the end of the dial and I couldn't move it anymore. Rhythm and blues tumbled out of WWRL over in Queens and the thumpin' and bumpin' of the music made my legs twitch.

Snapping the radio off, I tucked the warm set against my side and closed my eyes, happy with the expanded world of radio I had discovered.

* * *

Whenever our family ended a visit with my Aunt Adeline and Uncle Joe in Union City, New Jersey, I hoped Dad would drive home a special way. It was usually dark after we said goodbye and headed out in the Packard. How elated I became as my father turned off Route 3 after Secaucus.

The bumpy Paterson Plank Road cut through the Jersey swamps and wound past towers for New York radio stations. I sat up straight on the back seat and peered out the window. In the daylight, the trip was exciting, but at night, it was enchanting.

A transmitter building came into view first. A box sign on the side of the road was lit from within and illuminated black letters on a yellow background for WHN. In a field beyond, red lights dotted the sky on three slender towers of steel, the top ones flashing on and off to me as the car sped by.

Next, a tower stretched to the sky like an elongated diamond as it balanced on a large ball surrounded by a chain link fence. Wires keeping the tower straight disappeared into the dark swamp water. Above the door of a little building, red neon letters were lit. I leaned closer to the car window and mouthed them: W O V.

Dad drove up the hill at Carlstadt, and I counted the short towers for WBNX as if all of them wouldn't be there if I didn't. The four towers stood in a row and blinked red lights in a cockeyed rhythm.

Mom turned on the dashboard radio and Walter Winchell came in from WJZ. The commentator's voice grew louder as our car bounced onto Route 17 and drew closer to the station's giant tower at Lodi. *I wonder what magic that tower and others in the swamps will be sending to my bedroom radio when I get home.*

A BOY'S LIFE

I was nothing at all like a withdrawn child obsessed with radio. I rode my bike with Frankie Ketz to watch trains at the Erie Railroad station in Ridgewood, picked-up empty soda bottles with Joe Rector to collect two-penny refunds at Lukey's grocery store and had to mow the lawn in the summer before my father got home.

Saturday afternoon, when I joined my friends waiting at the top of Albert Place, was best. The orange and brown Inner City bus may have been old, but it whizzed up Laurel Road on solid black tires with yellow wooden spokes. The brakes gave a hiss of air when the bus stopped at the curb. As we climbed three steps into the long cab, the motor grumbled under a long snoot, and when the bus chugged away, clouds of white smoke billowed out the back.

We scattered along a narrow aisle between high-backed leather seats. I tried to beat everyone to one over a rear wheel, so I could sit with my feet on the hump and feel the vibration. When the bus got a block away from our destination, we all reached up at the same time and yanked the cord to buzz the driver to stop.

Hundreds of kids from all over Ridgewood and surrounding towns jammed into the Warner Theater for the

Saturday matinee. Soft seats flipped up as we stood to cheer when a rooster appeared on the screen to start the Warner Pathe newsreel. We waited quietly while a man with rimless glasses was introduced as the President of the United States. I was impressed with the bank of microphones in front of him, lettered with the initials of networks: CBS, NBC and MBS. A scene followed with somber men in dark suits and uniforms signing a book on the deck of a battleship. The newsreel ended, Bugs Bunny's face appeared, and we cheered again.

"Ah, what's up, doc?" he said munching a carrot and a Looney Tunes cartoon began.

After *Previews of Coming Attractions*, we were treated to two – count 'em, – two feature-length movies. The whole show cost thirty-five cents, which left enough from my allowance to buy a bag of Planter's Salted Peanuts at the concession stand.

If we didn't like what was playing, we'd throw peanuts and sticky candy at the screen. The projector would stop, the lights would come on and the diminutive manager would confront us from the stage.

"You kids better settle down or I'll clear ya all outta here!" Mr. Costa would shout. We'd shut up, the lights would go off and the screen would light up again.

Because I studied whatever photos I could find about radio, I knew that a scene in one movie wasn't right. It was set in a studio, and a round microphone – the type used for public address systems at ball parks – was up by the announcer's forehead. He read a news bulletin about an escaped criminal by yelling. In a window behind him, a man fiddled with a wall of equipment.

"That's not the way it really looks," I harrumphed and sat back in my seat.

Before starting to a matinee one Saturday, I was told by my mother that I was not to stay for the second movie. She didn't tell me then, but it was based on a steamy novel from her *Book of the Month Club*.

"You're to leave right after the first one."

When it began, I stayed in my seat as the title appeared: "The Postman Always Rings Twice." The credits started, and I backed up the aisle. As the first scene came on, I ran to the lobby and peeked around the door. When the actors began to speak, I dashed out of the theater.

* * *

I sneaked into my parents' bedroom and pulled a cardboard sheet from the waste basket. Before wrapping Dad's white shirts in cellophane, Bon Ton Cleaners inserted the sheets to keep them stiff. After he dressed for work, I got something to scribble on. I liked to draw.

Sitting at the metal table in the kitchen, I dumped out stubby pencils and broken crayons from an empty coffee can. I drew mostly B-17s pasting cities, bombs falling from their bellies like columns of eggs. Still, my parents fanned the small flame of artistic talent they saw in me.

Dad brought a table up from his workshop in the basement. He fastened the top to the frame with hinges, so it could be set at different angles.

"It's called an easel," he said.

Dad carried the bulky thing upstairs and placed it in the unfinished portion of the attic. Mom followed with paint, brushes, charcoal sticks, and a sketch pad. Under the glare of a light bulb hanging from the ceiling, the room became an artist's garret. With bold strokes of charcoal on the sketch pad, I copied heads of characters from comic books. I drew my brother with Porky Pig's nose, but crumpled up the paper before he saw it. I splashed colors from pots of poster paint to show planes in a dog fight over France. Swirling a wet brush on a tray of watercolor tablets, I painted cows grazing by a barn. Squeezing tubes of oil paint on a wooden palette, I held it by the thumbhole and smeared globs on a piece of canvas stretched on a frame. The bowl of fruit I created had shrunken oranges and odd-shaped pears.

After a month of dabbling, my passion to be on the radio was stronger than pursuing a life in the art world. Laying the top of the easel flat, I cut out a square with one of Dad's saws and inserted my brother's record changer to create a radio station. My parents were angry when they saw what I had done, but they realized where I was heading at age nine.

* * *

The day Dad caught me fooling with the record changer in the altered easel, I was scared, but he surprised me with a story about radio in his youth.

"A buddy and I rigged up a receiver so we could listen to Morse code. We swapped the earphones to hear signals between ships and the New York harbor master. One night, he tore off them off, and said 'My God, voices!' He had picked up the first message using microphones."

I had heard the "dit-dit-da-dit" of Morse code at the beginning of an RKO movie and figured microphones had been around since the beginning of radio. My father taught me otherwise.

* * *

On summer afternoons when it was too hot to do anything, I opened the window upstairs to let in a breeze and flopped on my bed. Turning on the radio, I tuned to WINS, and Mel Allen's voice put me right inside Yankee Stadium.

My imagination pictured the foul lines of white lime stretching from home plate to the bleachers. Though the brown dirt of the diamond was chewed-up by the players' spikes, lush green grass with no dandelions lay as smooth as a soft, green carpet all the way out to the black scoreboard rising high in center field. I could see fans with their shirt sleeves rolled up, clutching wax cups filled with beer and yelling at the umpires. At the crack of a bat, Mel Allen shouted.

"It's a short hopper to Rizzuto! He throws to second. Williams slides!" I saw powder explode from the bag as the runner's foot slammed into it. "And he's out!"

The crowd cheered, and I imagined Ted Williams getting up, brushing dirt off his uniform and trotting back to the Red Sox dugout.

On the sandlot at Kenilworth Elementary, I imitated Mel Allen tying his cigar and beer sponsors to a Yankee game. I shouted that a home run was either a "White Owl Wallop" or a "Ballantine Blast."

If a batted ball sailed all the way to the chain-link fence on Pleasant Avenue, I yelled like Russ Hodges did when the Camel sign at the Polo Grounds was hit in a Giants game.

"Cartons of Camel Cigarettes are going out to the veterans' hospital in Massapequa, Long Island!"

As I waited for my turn at bat, I stood behind the backstop and pretended I was Red Barber calling balls and strikes in a Dodger game from his "Catbird Seat" at Ebbets Field. Boys at home plate would turn around and yell.

"Shut up, Archard!"

In the summer, buses took my buddies and me from the Elk's Club in Ridgewood to games in New York City. At the ball parks in the Bronx and Brooklyn, I looked up at the row of press boxes to locate the radio booths. They were easy to spot because banners hung from open windows for WINS at Yankee Stadium, WMCA at the Polo Grounds and WHN at Ebbets Field. *I wish I could be up there, sitting next to the play-by-play man at the microphone.*

WHN did something unique if a Dodger game was threatened by rain. It had Borsht Belt comedian Morey Amsterdam stand by at the station with two singers and a band. If the action was held up at the ballpark, the group in the studio filled in with comedy and songs until the sun came out. They were called "The Gloom Dodgers."

Some afternoons I actually hoped it would rain as Amsterdam made me laugh with his patter of gags and put-downs. He sang a silly song I taught my friends at school.

"We've got a hen down on our farm as lazy as lazy can be.

She lays seven eggs every five days. She likes her weekends free.

Yuck-a-puck. Yuck-a-puck. Yuck-a-puck, yuck-a-puck, yuck-a-puck."

RADIO ALL WEEK LONG

Afternoons at five o'clock, my brother and I ran in the house and rushed past Mom in the kitchen as her last soap opera ended. She dutifully clicked off the radio on the counter, and Tom and I took positions at the big Zenith in the living room. For the next hour, we sat cross-legged on the rug and didn't say a word as our favorite adventure serials came on one after another. We threw fingers to see who'd get up at the end of a fifteen-minute episode to turn the dial from WOR to WJZ and back again. I knew I hadn't missed a thing when noise and yelling started each program.

A plane dove with a roar, a clock chimed, and an announcer called out *"Captaaain Midniiight!"*

A Chinese gong rang and a voice shouted *"Terrrry and the Pirates!"*

I heard whistling wind and a deep voice bellow "On, King! On, you huskies!" and knew *Sergeant Preston of the Yukon* was coming on.

Toward the end of the hour, a quartet sang "Have you triiied Wheaties?" and, *Jack Armstrong, All American Boy* stepped up to continue his adventure.

Mom couldn't help but hear the serials while she fixed dinner. When the sponsors' products in the cupboard were used, she saved the box tops and labels so Tom and I could mail away for offers on the programs. The day a brown padded envelope arrived from the advertiser of *Captain Midnight*, Mom greeted us as we came home from school.

"You boys got something in the mail today."

My brother ripped open the envelope and shook out a shiny metal decoder ring.

"Let me see it," I said.

"Be careful," he said. "Don't break it."

The ring was mounted by two small wheels on top of each other. One was embossed with letters and the other engraved with numbers. We left the ring on top of the big radio until *Captain Midnight* was broadcast on Friday.

Before the announcer signed off, he gave a series of numbers and Tom copied them down. When the code word was given, Tom twisted the small wheel with numbers to the corresponding letters to spell out a message. He wrote the words and sat back.

"What do they say?" I asked.

"Ovaltine builds strong bones," he said and crinkled his nose in disgust.

* * *

My mother assigned chores to be done on each school night.

"Either bring dirty dishes from the table to the sink or stand and dry." I fought with Tom every evening to see who'd get the quicker job.

"You cleared the table last night. It's my turn."

Once the dishes were done, I had to sit at the kitchen table and practice writing cursive letters or wrestle with arithmetic. I kept looking at the clock above the stove as all the good programs started at eight. *I'm in prison, and my mother is the warden.*

After homework, I ran upstairs for the final chores of getting into pajamas and brushing teeth. At last, I jumped in bed and turned on the radio.

Foot steps, gun shots, sinister music and murderers streamed in above my pillow followed by laughter, singing, applause and people with funny voices.

Inner Sanctum began with a door opening on squeaky hinges and a man speaking in a spooky voice.

"Good evening…friends?" *He doesn't sound like a friend to me.*

A show started with an announcer shouting a bunch of odd names.

"The Johnson's Wax Program with Fibber McGee and Molly!"

I said the names out loud one week and my brother looked over at me from his bed and frowned.

Another program came on quietly with a wife and husband talking like Mom and Dad.

"Another cup of Maxwell coffee, George?"

"Sure, Gracie. Pour me one."

One began with a telephone ringing followed by an introduction I memorized word for word and recited on the schoolyard: "Hello, Duffy's Tavern, where the elite meet to eat. Duffy ain't here. Archie the manager speakin'. Oh, hullo Duffy."

Characters on programs had names like Boston Blackie, Baby Snooks and Parkya Karkus. *I wonder what name I'll have when I get on the radio?*

Every Monday night at nine, goosebumps would rise on my arms when an announcer yelled.

"Lux … presents Hollywood!"

A harp swept in, an audience burst into applause, and I imagined the silver-haired host I saw in Mom's *Radio Mirror* stepping up to a microphone. In his eloquent delivery, Cecil B. DeMille told me what I was going to hear.

"Tonight, our staaahs, Dana Andrews and Gene Tierney, appear in the radio adaptation of *Laura*." For the next hour, screen actors recreated a movie in sound only, but I supplied the action in my mind's eye. I usually fell asleep before *Lux Radio Theater* ended, so Tom had to turn off my radio before he turned off his light.

At breakfast after a *Lux* broadcast the night before, my mother told of a family connection.

"Your Uncle Jack is married to the woman who writes the commercials for that program," she said. Mom's brother, Jack Davidson, remarried after my Aunt Emily died. I liked visiting them when she was alive. Their home looked like an English manor sitting up a hill in upscale Upper Montclair, New Jersey, a blue four-door LaSalle parked in the two-car garage. Uncle Jack's new wife worked for the advertising agency for Lux Soap. I never met her, but felt important that I had a link to the radio business.

Gangbusters came on with the sound of breaking glass, a burglar alarm, a car speeding away and the ratta-tat-tat of a machine gun. The announcer concluded the program each week with an announcement.

"Be on the lookout for," he'd begin then give a name, description, and list of crimes for one of the ten "most wanted" men in America. His closing, always the same, was frightening: "This person is armed and considered dangerous." When he said that, I pulled the covers up higher and imagined the fugitive climbing in the bedroom window.

Friday nights, I struggled to stay awake after the comedies and mysteries ended to hear faint laughter and clinking of glasses before an announcer spoke.

"Good evening, ladies and gentlemen. From the beautiful Grill Room of the Hotel Taft in downtown Times Square New York, we bring you the scintillating rhythms of Vincent Lopez and his orchestra."

When the clapping and music started, I pictured men in tuxedos and women in slinky gowns putting down glasses of champagne and gliding out on the floor to dance.

* * *

Radio didn't let up on the weekend. Saturday mornings, *Let's Pretend* whisked me off to lands of fairy tales on a magic carpet or the hump of a camel. A rocket ship blasted me to distant planets on *Space Patrol*, and I was tickled with the conversations between the characters on *Big Jon and Sparky*. Sparky spoke in a revved-up voice and was the little pal to Jon with the normal voice. My brother read that Sparky's parts were recorded by Jon on discs and played back at a faster speed.

"He has to time his responses, so it sounds like he and Sparky are talking to each other."

After Tom told me that, I marveled at how the program was done.

If I didn't go to the movies Saturday afternoon, I waited for a program that began with a wailing train whistle, speeding locomotive and an announcer speaking with all the drama he could muster: "A silver meteor races toward the city at a hundred miles an hour, flashes by rows of tenements at 125th Street, then dives with a roar into the tunnel beneath Park Avenue to arrive at Grand Central Station – crossroads of a million private lives. A stage on which are played a thousand dramas daily."

The next morning when Mom yelled upstairs to get dressed for Sunday school, I snapped on the radio to hear a man sing: "Oh, I'm the Comic Weekly Man, the jolly Comic Weekly Man, and I'm here to read the funnies to you happy boys and honeys."

The "funnies" were the color comics in the Sunday *Journal American*. Youngsters spread out the pages and had fun following the "Comic Weekly Man" along as he described the action in the panels and read the words in the balloons. Because Dad had the *Herald Tribune* delivered to our house Sunday without any comics, I felt left out. However, my vivid imagination let me see Pop Eye, Dick Tracy, Little Annie Rooney and the rest.

After lunch, the Moline Sisters sang on WOR. I joined in singing their theme song and Mom and Dad did, too: "Marching along to-geee-ther, hand in hand for H-O Oats."

I wondered about the sisters. *How old are they? Do they go to school? Are their parents looking adoringly at them through the slanted windows of the studio?*

"Who are the Moline Sisters?" I asked my folks.

"They're two kids whose pushy parents are forcing them to sing for money," my father said. I supposed he was recalling how he was taken out of school by his mother and put to work when he was a youth.

The Molines were followed by a program that gave me the creeps. There was no talking after the announcer introduced it, just canaries chirping to an organ for fifteen minutes. I pictured an old white-haired lady hunched over a keyboard in her apartment, shades drawn, the air thick with cooking odors. Against a wall, dozens of small yellow birds imprisoned in wire cages dug their claws into narrow perches and whistled and trilled to the notes pressed out by the woman's bony fingers.

Another program that started with sinister warbling from an organ came on later in the afternoon. This one did have talking as a man spoke, and he sounded like he was talking through a telephone. I loved to recite what he said for anyone who'd listen, pinching my nose together to get the right effect: "Who knows what evil lurks in the hearts of men. The Shadow knows. Heh, heh, heh, heh, heh, heh, heeeh."

The more I listened to the radio, the more I became impressed with the announcers. They put smiles in their voices to bring on comedy shows and dropped their pitch low to introduce a murder mystery. In the middle of shows, they would read the commercials with sincerity then at the end state the name of the network with pride. I imitated the accents of actors playing tough guys from Brooklyn and cowboys out West, but the announcers didn't have accents that indicated where they came from. Every word they spoke was crisp and clear exactly how Miss May insisted I speak when reading out loud in her class. Before, I'd wanted to be a character with a funny voice, but I changed my mind. I wanted to be an announcer.

The next time I went to the library at Kenilworth Elementary, I took down the heavy *R* book from the shelf of encyclopedias and looked up "Radio." It taught me about Marconi and his wireless, de Forrest and his vacuum tube, and how Mr. Sarnoff and Mr. Paley started their networks. When I pulled Mom's *Radio Mirror* from the magazine rack at home, I didn't just look at the pictures – I began to read the articles.

Before long, when I rode home on my bike after being peppered with a baseball on the sandlot, I shouted like the announcer on Monday night.

"Lux ...presents Hollywood!"

IT'S ELEMENTARY

I pouted on the bus all the way down to Sears Roebuck in Hackensack, New Jersey. My mother dragged me to shop for clothes before fifth grade started in the fall of 1946. The trip was an ordeal for me and for Mom, too.

The Sears store was constructed of big, dull gray blocks of concrete piled one on top of another. Square columns at each corner made the building look like a prison. Going into the place with my mother, I hoped none of my friends were there to see me.

Riding the escalator to the boys' department in the basement, I was met by the odd smell of new shirts and pants mixed with the aroma of popcorn cooking somewhere.

Mannequins with bland expressions on their plaster faces stood in awkward poses with the latest back-to-school outfits on their stiff bodies. I shuffled behind my mother then slouched in the aisle as she held a shirt to my chest.

"Stand up straight, David. I want to see how much you've grown."

The plaid flannel shirts Mom bought were okay, but the pants were another thing.

At play, I got to wear blue denim dungarees with metal rivets on the pockets and a leather patch in the back saying

"Levi's." I was happy when rips appeared in the knees, because that showed I was one of the rough and tumble kids on the block. To attend Kenilworth Elementary School, however, I had to wear knickers.

The dumb billowy pants were held tight below my knees by elastic bands sewn inside. The black corduroy whistled when I walked, and if the knickers got wet on rainy days, the fabric chafed the inside of my tender legs. I had to wear long black stockings, too, but in the spring I rolled them down to my shoes at recess. I hated knickers, but I wasn't embarrassed to wear them. All the boys at Kenilworth wore them.

Mom's choice of shoes didn't vary. On Saturdays and in the summer, I wore a spiffy pair of high-top sneakers with the red *Keds* ball on each ankle. For school, though, my mother always bought me a pair of *Thom McAn Boy Scout Shoes*. They were heavy, brown, clunky shoes with rounded toes and thick rubber soles. I felt like a clod-hopper in a farm field when I clomped around in them. But there was one neat thing about the shoes when I wore them – I could kick a soccer ball the length of the school playground.

* * *

I liked the two-story stone school building on Kenilworth Avenue and the teachers, most of them older than my mother. I liked sitting at a wooden desk and feeling the initials carved on top. I liked the smell of books with worn covers and doodles drawn inside by students long gone.

If the streets were dry or free of ice, I rode my bike to school arriving in plenty of time for Bible reading and the Pledge of Allegiance. In the morning, subjects went by fast as we learned vocabulary words, figured arithmetic problems and searched the pink, blue and green countries on the shiny world map on the wall.

At lunch time, I rushed home for the sandwich Mom had ready. After I ate, she made me swallow a teaspoon of cod liver oil before I jumped on my bike and raced back to school. I didn't want to miss joining a large gang in a no-holds-barred game of soccer against the big sixth-graders before the bell rang for the afternoon session to begin.

My reputation for entertaining classmates must have preceded me into the fifth grade because Mrs. Murphy, the teacher, gave me something to say in the Thanksgiving pageant. Thrilled with being chosen, I worked on it right away.

In the seclusion of my bedroom, I said my line, first like wisecracking Charlie McCarthy, then like bombastic Senator Claghorn, and finally like Archie from Brooklyn on *Duffy's Tavern*.

"Who're you talking to?" Mom called up the stairs.

Finally, I decided to drop the idea of being a character and just be myself.

The pageant was held the week of Thanksgiving. My folks sat on wooden folding chairs with other parents in the auditorium. I sat cross-legged on the stage with the rest of the fifth grade to portray a family gathered for dinner. Pat Chilton, playing the role of the mom, wore an apron that wrapped around her like a skirt, and Harold Meyers, playing the dad, had on a tie that went down to his knees. They told the story of the Pilgrims' voyage to the New World, and when they got to the part about being crowded on the Mayflower, I piped up with my big line: "Boy, they must have been packed in there like sardines!"

Laughter from the audience sent the tingling sensation through me, only that night it was different. *I'm entertaining grown-ups!*

* * *

One morning in winter, our family woke to eighteen inches of snow on the ground. A city plow had come down the street and pushed a mound across the driveway. My father pulled on a pair of black galoshes over his shoes and fastened them with metal buckles. After shoveling the snow mound, he backed the Packard from the garage and fastened a set of chains around the rear tires. When he left for work, the car rattled and thumped all the way up Albert Place.

Tom and I sat at the cold metal kitchen table and warmed our hands over steaming bowls of Maltex. My mother wrapped her bathrobe tightly around her and leaned out the kitchen door. Brushing snow from the wooden box at the steps, she brought in bottles of milk. The frigid temperature made cream at the top burst through the paper caps and stand in stubby pale yellow cores. I watched as they thawed on the counter and slid back in.

When Mom turned on the radio, John Gambling came in from WOR and he was announcing school closings. My ears perked up, and my brother laid down his spoon and shushed me.

"Our schools may be on the list," he said in a whisper.

Gambling announced closings in the five boroughs of New York just as tan slices of bread popped up in the toaster. I spread jelly on mine and chewed quietly so I wouldn't miss any schools.

"Be careful," my mother said. "Make sure he says Ridgewood, New Jersey, schools and not the Ridgewood over in Queens."

Gambling announced closings for Westchester County. My brother twirled a glass of orange juice, and Mom joined us at the table with a cup of coffee. At last, he read closings for north Jersey.

"All schools in Bergen County are closed."

Tom and I cheered and Mom sighed. We ran upstairs, got dressed and headed outside to ride our sleds all day.

*   *   *

One afternoon in the spring of 1946, the janitor at Kenilworth Elementary cleared away the folding chairs in the auditorium, and it became the Roseland Ballroom. My mother wanted me to learn the social niceties that went with dancing, so I was out on the floor with the rest of the kids with my hands washed and hair combed.

Mr. and Mrs. Geiger arrived from their dance studio in Ridgewood, and the husband placed a portable record machine on the edge of stage. The Geigers faced each other, showed us how to hold our partners and then demonstrated the boxy steps of something they called the "foxtrot."

Mr. Geiger started a record on the machine, and an orchestra played "That Old Devil Moon." The couple swept out on the floor, spun around to each other, and began to dance.

Mr. Geiger wore a tan suit with a yellow scarf bunched around his neck. His soft brown shoes glided across the worn floor of the auditorium as though he were weightless. Mrs. Geiger, her hair flowing free, wore a red skirt that swirled around her legs. When the music ended, she kicked up one of her black high-heel shoes, put her head back and laughed. *How smooth and confident they look.*

The Geigers had my buddies and me line up on one side of the auditorium and the girls line up on the other. Mrs. Geiger stood in the middle of the floor. "The proper way for a gentleman to ask a lady to dance," she said, "is to walk over to her and say 'May I have this dance?'"

Then Mrs. Geiger moved out of the way and, at her command, the boys dashed over to the girls. I elbowed Malcolm George to get to one of the girls I liked. I mumbled my request to Carolyn Krause, and she walked out on the floor with me stumbling behind her.

We stood face to face, and Carolyn put her right hand in the palm of my upraised left one. She rested her other hand on my shoulder. My right hand touched her waist, and I discovered how soft she was. When we came closer to dance, I found out how good she smelled.

The orchestra on the record machine started to play again, and the two of us moved with stiff legs to the foxtrot. I kept looking down at my feet to get the steps right. *I wish I could twirl Carolyn around like Fred Astaire does with Ginger Rogers in the movies.*

For the next hour, the Geigers played records with different rhythms and went back on the floor to demonstrate other steps. I watched the couple intently to learn the moves until the boys were told to ask the girls to dance again. I waltzed and cha-cha'd around the auditorium with other girls and discovered they were just as soft as Carolyn.

When it was a girl-ask-boy dance, Edith Haldane came over to me. "May I have this dance?" she asked, her eyes looking down, a slight smile on her lips.

I didn't admit it to my buddies, but I enjoyed the dance lesson. When I got home, I told my mother about the experience including the dances with girls. "If you don't stop biting your nails," she warned me, "girls won't have anything to do with you."

I stopped biting right then.

THE BOOK

A flat heavy package, different than the wrapped toys, had my name on it under the Christmas tree. I tore off the bright paper and was met by the dark orange cover of a hardback book. I held it up.

"Oh, boy!" I pushed away the other presents and began to read.

Radio, the Fifth Estate was written by a woman in the Chicago office of the National Broadcasting Company. Judith Waller used words I'd never seen, but her writing opened the inner workings of the radio business. I learned a microphone changed sound waves to electrical impulses. Sent on a telephone wire to a station's transmitter, the impulses were radiated from a steel tower to receivers in homes and changed back to sound waves.

To my amazement, programs just didn't happen. Scripts had to be written for the actors including indications of sound effects to aid the action and musical bridges to move one scene to another. My biggest discovery was that sponsorships of programs were sold to advertisers to pay for writers, directors, engineers and air talent.

"So that's how I'll be paid to be an announcer," I said under my breath.

"What?" my brother said vaguely as he continued to unwrap a chemistry set.

I flipped to the scant number of black-and-white photos in the back of the book. One showed a studio at NBC, and I pictured myself seated under the microphone that hung above a table. With script in hand, I looked through the slanted window of the control room, waiting for a cue to be thrown to me before I talked to millions of listeners coast to coast.

I spent the rest of Christmas Day with my nose buried in the book.

* * *

One chapter showed a daily schedule used by WFAA in Dallas. Information divided in columns showed the titles of programs, times on and off for each, advertisers, the studios they came from and which announcers were assigned. Fascinated, I had to create a schedule for my own imaginary station.

After lifting the heavy black Royal typewriter out of the living room closet, I set it on the card table, rolled in a sheet of paper and pecked the keys one at a time.

My station was given the call letters W D A V. When I typed them, I left a space between each letter for emphasis and sat back. *Pretty clever.*

Beginning on the next line, I typed the name of a program I listened to at night, *Casey, Crime Photographer.* I wasn't sure if I spelled the word "photographer" right. Pulling on my knowledge of advertisers, I typed in "Ovaltine." My choice of studio was easy - it received the letter A. The right hand margin was approaching, and I wanted to squeeze in the name of announcer Andre Baruch. I didn't know how to spell his name, so I typed "Al Bart" instead.

I made mistakes typing and found it tough to erase a letter, so I stopped after the first line. According to my hardcover book, I had done the work of a "traffic director" at a radio station. *I think I'll stick with having fun as an announcer instead of slaving away directing traffic.* At least, that was my plan at the time.

FIRST TRY

Flipping the pages of Dad's *Popular Science* magazine, the word "radio" caught my eye in a headline. An article told of an experimental station located in Alpine, New Jersey. The owner was experimenting with a way to broadcast a signal that couldn't be affected by static. He called it "frequency modulation" or "FM" for short.

A photo showed the station's tower perched above the Hudson River on the edge of the Palisades. With three steel arms sticking out at the top of four thick legs, it looked like a weird scarecrow. Even the call letters were strange. Alpine wasn't far from Ridgewood, so I planned a bike hike because I wanted to find KE2XCC.

On a bright spring morning, Frankie Ketz and I struck out across the green fields of Bergen County. The magazine said the station was north of the George Washington Bridge. Reaching the Hudson River, we began a roller coaster ride on a blacktop highway cut into the granite of the Palisades. We pumped up steep rises and coasted down deep dips until I spotted steel arms looming over trees ahead. Braking to a stop, I knew it was the tower for KE2XCC.

A chain-link fence ten feet tall surrounded the grounds, and a large padlock secured the gate. We laid our bikes down, dropped on hands and knees, and I parted a tangle of bushes with my hands.

At the base of the tower was a plain stone building that looked like a shoe box with windows. I imagined the owner of KE2XCC inside, wearing a lab coat and goggles, grinning and rubbing his hands together as glowing coils crackled and hissed around him.

"I don't think we oughta climb over the fence to get in," I said to Frankie. "We might get shot at if we did."

Dejected, I picked up my bike, turned it around and with my friend behind me, rode the highway roller coaster home.

* * *

I tried to soak up as much information as I could about radio. Besides the hard cover book I kept on the shelf above my pillow, there was the "R" volume of the encyclopedias in the school library and Mom's *Radio Mirror* from the A & P. The mailman delivered *Popular Science* every month and I grabbed the *Radio Guide* from the *Herald Tribune* on Sundays. If I managed to find any photos, they weren't enough to satisfy my hunger. I wanted to see studios for real.

The time I twisted the dial on my bedroom radio to find all stations available, I remembered landing on a loud one. The station was in a city close to Ridgewood and down the line of the Erie Railroad, so I convinced my friend Frankie to ride the rails with me. "We're going to Paterson and find a radio station."

I was surprised to see the station listed in the slim Ridgewood telephone book that Mom kept under the cradle phone in the kitchen. Under the W's, one simple line read "WPAT, 66 Hamilton St., Paterson." With school out for the summer in 1948, Frankie and I had all day for the venture. Pooling our allowance money, we took the orange and brown bus downtown.

In the Erie station house, we bought round-trip tickets from a man behind a window with bars. We ran out on the platform as an eastbound train pulled in from Ho Ho Kus and a conductor swung off a Pullman car in a cloud of steam.

"Where're you headed?" I asked.

"Paterson," he barked.

Frankie and I climbed aboard the first car, empty of passengers. Sitting on the edge of a hard leather-covered bench, I explained to him why I asked the conductor for the destination.

"My Dad says there's a switch down the line that sends trains to Jersey City or Paterson and beyond. I don't know how far that one goes, but I rode it once with Mom to visit Grandma and we got as far as Montclair."

Anxious for the train to get moving, I drummed my fingers on my knees.

C'mon. I've got a radio station to find.

At last, the conductor called out from the platform: "Boarrrd!"

A short blast sounded from the whistle on the locomotive, and I leaned into the aisle hoping to see the engineer in the cab through the open door, but the view was blocked by the black backside of the coal car.

Because I'd watched trains start before, I knew what was happening. When the brakes were released with a hiss of steam, the locomotive belched once, then twice. Its giant steel wheels spun and grabbed the rails, and with great huffs and puffs from the front of the train, the Pullman car lurched forward and began to move. I looked at Frankie and we both laughed with excitement. As the train eased away from the station, I scooted to a smeared window on the other side of the aisle to see if I recognized anything on the west side of town. I caught a glimpse of the office for our family dentist perched on a hill. When I sat in Dr. Burns' chair, I could see trains come and go at the station and wondered how great it would be ride one. *Now I am!*

Through Slanted Windows

The train picked up speed and I rushed back to the bench. Looking out at the east side, I could barely see the back of the A & P hidden behind boxes and crates stacked along a fence. Grilles of cars flashed in the sun at Higgins Buick. I got a quick look at the three-story apartment house where Frankie and I had seen the Negro kids playing, fire escapes running down the back of the building in a column of Z's. Wind rushed through the Pullman car, and before I could catch my breath, houses and trees lined both sides of the tracks and the train was slowing down for Glen Rock.

After a stop at Hawthorne, the scenery turned harsh. I gaped at shirts and pants pinned to ropes between tenement buildings. At crossing gates, trailer trucks covered with road grime waited, snorting black exhaust as we sailed by.

As the train started up the grade to Paterson, we passed an old brick factory. It was crowned with a rusty water tank, and faded letters spelled "Haband Clothing for Men." Nearby, a fortress-like building of cinderblocks and glass-block windows bore a sign that said the place made ladies undergarments by Barbizon. Soon, the train glided into the elevated platform at the city's green steel Erie Railroad station. From the Marcal Paper plant to the east, streams of cars, trucks and buses sped underneath. I looked across the aisle to the west.

Paterson, New Jersey, was built against a dark, lumpy mountain. Smokestacks and warehouses spread out from faded office buildings packed in the center of the city. Mrs. Murphy, our fifth grade teacher, had told us there was a museum on the mountain that we should visit with our parents. But on that day, Frankie and I didn't need our folks along – we were two daring eleven-year-old lads out on an adventure of our own. We jumped off the train and ran downstairs to the terminal waiting room.

At a row of telephone booths, I lifted a heavy directory hanging from a chain and flipped through the pages to find a map for Paterson. My finger circled the tangle of streets.

Bingo! A double line labeled "Hamilton Street" went out from the center.

"C'mon, Frankie," I said, closing the directory. "I know exactly where we're going."

Our young legs strode into the confusion of downtown. Horns honked and people rushed past on stained sidewalks. Waiting at a corner for a traffic light to change, Frankie poked me and pointed up to a sign: "Hamilton St." *Just where the map told me it would be!*

As we turned on Hamilton Street, my steps quickened. Starting up a hill, I began to run and my friend followed. When the sidewalk leveled off, I saw what I'd been seeking. Across from the dull grey walls of the Passaic County Court House, a modern office building glistened in the sun. With heart racing, I ran to it so fast that a flock of pigeons flew off the statues at the court house. On the right half of the ground floor were two tall windows and a glass door backed by tightly closed blinds. Sharp red letters trimmed in gold on both windows spelled "WPAT 930 on Your Dial." The words were exciting yet daunting. My hand didn't reach for the door. "Uh, maybe we ought to go in another way," I said to Frankie.

We went to the double doors under the number "66" and peeked in. No one was in the lobby to chase us away, so we went in and tip-toed down a marble hall. At another glass door and windows with lettering for the station, we halted. I could hear the ringing of a telephone and the clacking of a typewriter behind closed blinds, but I didn't open the door.

"Frankie, no grown-ups are gonna let two kids come in and look around. Let's go home."

Starting back down Hamilton Street, I spied an alley on the side of the building and held up my hand.

"Wait here," I told Frankie. He watched from the sidewalk as I stumbled over rocks and empty bottles to get to an open window.

Through the window, I could hear a rapid chunka-chunka-chunka sound and the ding of a bell. I knew it was a teletype machine from having seen one in a movie, and I pictured it rocking on four legs as it hammered out news from around the world. For a moment, I leaned my back against the building and looked at the sky. How exciting it was to be so close to radio.

* * *

Although my father spent his adult life working with his head, I think he would have been happier working with his hands. Hammers, pliers, and screwdrivers hung on pegboard in his workshop in the basement along with a blue Craftsman band saw, lathe, and drill press that were bolted to the sturdy work bench he'd built. On the workshop floor lay curlicues of wood shavings and piles of sawdust. He'd be down there most weekends sawing and nailing something for my mother.

Using his ingenuity, and instructions out of *Popular Science*, my father converted the speaker from an old radio so it could transmit the human voice. He inserted it in a small wooden box, covered the opening with the scrap of thin rug and screwed it on a fancy pedestal turned out on the lathe. His creation became my first microphone. Dad allowed my brother and me to set up a radio studio next to the oil burner. One Saturday, Tom brought a card table down from the living room, and I placed the ponderous microphone on it. He then took a long strand of wire from the mike, ran it upstairs and attached it to the back of the radio in the kitchen. Mom and Dad sat up there and listened while Tom and I huddled below.

We had scribbled a rough script for a cops and robbers show on school notebook paper. After a brief rehearsal, we dropped the idea of using a kazoo and harmonica for the opening theme.

"They sound corny," Tom said, and I agreed. When we were ready for our performance, he yelled upstairs to our folks: "Here it comes!"

Sitting shoulder to shoulder at the microphone, we played all the parts by using voices and dialects.

    Tom: (Irish cop) All right now, lad, put the gun down and come out with your hands up.

    Dave: (Tough gangster) Come in and get me, copper.

For the sound of car tires squealing to a stop, I screeched, "Eeeee!" For gun shots, Tom smacked a metal trash can with a stick: "Bang, bang-bang!" Halfway through, we paused for a commercial.

    Dave: Our play is brought to you by Rheingold Beer.

    Both: (Singing) My beer is Rheingold, the dry beer.
            Think of Rheingold whenever you buy beer.
            It's not bitter, not sweet. It's the full-flavored treat.
            Won't you try extra dry Rheingold Beer?

We heard laughter upstairs.

My father went next door and dragged a neighbor over to the house. Big and round with a bushy moustache, Lou Van Delden was a patrolman with the Village of Ridgewood Police Department. The two men joined Mom, drank cans of Rheingold and listened as Tom and I chased villains on the radio. Coming upstairs after our broadcast, we were shocked to see a real policeman sitting in the kitchen.

Dad got a kick out of a line in our program, and he repeated it often: "Down the alley, O'Malley!"

THE TOUR

My father's announcement at dinner made milk come up my nose.

"This Saturday for your birthday, we're going into New York and visit Radio City. How does that sound?"

"Really? You mean NBC? Oh, boy!"

Mom handed me my napkin.

* * *

I ran to the gray and silver overhang sticking out from the RCA Building on West 49th Street. Even in the morning sun, red neon letters were lit spelling "NBC STUDIOS." My parents caught up with me, and I pulled them by their hands.

Pushing through the revolving doors, I felt like a celebrity coming to do a broadcast. Strutting to the carpeted stairs leading to the network, I hoped the people waiting at the elevators saw me. *Maybe they'll think I'm a child actor here to star on a show.* I started to run up the stairs, but my father took hold of my shoulder. "Slow down, Dave."

The circular mezzanine for the National Broadcasting Company was ringed by a chrome railing and furnished with dark blue sofas and chairs where visitors waited for the tour.

While my parents sat down, I walked to a row of photographs on a maroon wall.

The head-and-shoulder photographs in black and white were portraits of stars I knew only by their names and voices. I looked at the round face of singer Kate Smith, then stepped sideways to see Bill Stern, the man who shouted on his Friday night *Sports Newsreel*. Newsman Morgan Beatty glared at me with a scowl. The photo of announcer Ben Grauer was the same one I saw on the cover of the Sunday *Radio Guide* and I recognized Bob Hope from his movies. The NBC family portraits ended with a jolt with the sourpuss of Fred Allen.

After I scanned the photographs, I noticed young men called "pages" rushing about in spiffy blue uniforms. *I bet they're running errands for the people on the wall.* An article in Mom's radio magazine had noted that singer Gordon McRae was an NBC page at Radio City before he sang on *The Bell Telephone Hour*. *Will I have to do that to get on the radio?*

When I heard the singing of Fred Waring and his Pennsylvanians come out of a speaker in the ceiling, I pictured them in a studio somewhere on floors above. Shivering with anticipation, I realized I was going to see live people gathered at actual microphones in real studios with slanted windows.

Before long, a woman in a blue uniform appeared and asked us to gather around her. I had figured it would be just me and my folks on the tour – my brother had something to do at home that day – so I was disappointed when other grown-ups and kids rose from sofas and chairs to join us.

"Hello, everyone, my name is Carol," the woman said. "Welcome to the National Broadcasting Company. I'll be your guide today. Please follow me as we begin our tour."

In an elevator with another family, I inspected their little boy's Bugs Bunny necktie and he stared my red bow tie. In the forties, even kids dressed up to go into the city.

Through Slanted Windows

The door slid closed, and the elevator started up to the labyrinth of NBC studios. There were no bright lights or angels singing, but I felt I was being raised to radio heaven.

After we crowded into a viewing room, Carol disappeared. She reappeared in a small studio on the other side of a slanted window. Standing at a microphone by a pile of gadgets on a table, she spoke over a speaker: "See if you can identify these sounds."

She banged a sheet of metal with a mallet, and I jumped as a clap of thunder from a summer rainstorm shot out. She bounced halves of coconut shells against her body, and I heard a horse pounding along a dusty trail. Tapping a frame of pegs up and down on the table, she made me imagine soldiers marching to battle. The group "ooo'd" and "ahhh'd" at each demonstration, and I thought of my brother and me doing the cops and robbers show back home. My screeching for brakes and Tom smacking a can for gunshots were nothing compared to the sophisticated sound effects at NBC.

Next, Carol led us down a hall to a thick door she pushed open easily with one hand. We followed her in and were met by an identical door a few steps beyond. She pushed it open and we entered a studio.

"You just passed through a sound lock," she said. "The double doors keep noise in the hall from leaking into the on-air activity in here."

The studio was about the size of our living room. In the middle was a black-top table with shiny metal edges, and a chair on wheels pulled up to it. An organ sat in the corner. *I wonder which of Mom's soap operas come from here.* Carol didn't say.

A microphone hung over the table, the black wire from it coiled along a pipe, wound down to three legs spread on the floor and snaked its way to a plug in the wall.

"That's a 'boom mike,'" Carol said. "It's suspended over the table so it can't be bumped by a person working underneath with a script and a cup of coffee." *If only I could sit under that mike for a moment and pretend my voice is going out on the air.*

"Notice the window of the adjoining control room," Carol continued. "The slanting of the window into the studio cuts the glare on the glass from lights in the ceiling. This allows the air talent in here to see vital hand signals from the director in the control room without distraction." I turned to my mother and whispered. "So that's why photos in your magazine show slanted windows."

Then Carol made a startling announcement.

"You are standing in a room-within-a-room! To reduce the rumble of subway trains under the building, all studios in Radio City are suspended by cables inside a larger chamber leaving a thin space around each one." Worried I might make the studio jiggle, I tip-toed across the floor as we left.

By now, I was out in front of the group and right behind Carol. I followed her into a booth and stepped up to a slanted window.

In a studio on the floor below, a group of men laughed as they lounged around a piano, drums and microphones. Carol said they were waiting to go on the air with *The Jack Berch Show*. I looked at my parents. "I know this program! I've listened to it!" I whispered. My mother nodded. She listened to it, too. The man's theme song was one of the many I had memorized.

"Are you listenin'? Are you whistlin'?
To this pretty little ditty that I'm singin' all in rhyme?"

I wondered which one in the group was Jack Berch. Carol pointed out a man with a small moustache who was seated on a stool with his jacket off.

"That's Jack Berch," she told us. "He doesn't use a prepared script, but makes his comments off the cuff. It's called 'ad-libbing' in radio." *I wonder if I'll be able to do that.*

In another elevator, I watched floor numbers flash 5, 6, 7, until they stopped on 8. I ran around the group and fell in step with Carol. At a set of double doors, she faced us and made an announcement with all the dramatics of an actress in a radio play.

"You are about to enter the largest radio studio in the world." She turned and pushed the doors open with both hands.

Studio 8H was far larger than the first one. In fact, it was twice as large as the Warner Theater in Ridgewood. Rows of red velvet seats anchored to the floor sloped down to a giant stage. Large pale yellow objects shaped like footballs and commas were attached to the walls.

"Those panels were designed specifically to aid the acoustics in this big studio," Carol said. *I guess if I yelled, I won't hear an echo.*

She noticed me looking at a set of shiny silver microphones hanging on thin wires from the ceiling.

"Those microphones are suspended over the audience to pick up reactions of laughter and applause," she explained.

Carol directed the group to look at the control room on the left of the stage. It was as big as our living room and my bedroom put together and took several sections of slanted windows to cover the opening. She drew in air and made her next pronouncement in one breath.

"The engineer operating the controls in *there* has to be careful the speakers that let the audience hear the performance in *here* don't interfere with the microphones feeding the program to the people at home." I let that fact sink in as she took another breath.

"If the speakers do interfere, a squeal called 'feedback' occurs." *My brain is swimming with all this stuff.*

Carol stepped out in front of us.

"On the grand stage before you," she said, her arm making a sweeping motion, "is where Arturo Toscanini will conduct the NBC Symphony later today and where Fred Allen will do his Sunday program tomorrow." My mouth hung open.

By seeing his photo in Mom's *Radio Mirror*, I imagined Toscanini swinging a baton, his frizzy white hair sticking out and his deep-set eyes penetrating each musician. I also pictured the characters lined up ready to talk to Mr. Allen – the old man from New England, the Irishman, the Southern senator and the Jewish lady. I didn't want to leave the majesty of Studio 8H, but Mom took me gently by the elbow.

The group was then taken two floors down and along a hallway. Through a long slanted window, I stared at men in shirtsleeves busy at typewriters. Their wire baskets overflowed with paper and clocks on the wall told them the time in London, Paris, Rome and Hong Kong.

"This is the NBC newsroom," Carol said, her voice hushed and serious.

I leaned closer to the window. Four teletype machines were rocking together on the other side, and I heard the chunka-chunka-chunka sound and dinging of their bells faintly through the glass.

Carol told us to look at a small booth along the back wall.

"A newsman can break in to any program from there with a bulletin," she said. *I can't wait to do that when I get on the air.*

A short man with a black goatee got up from his desk and walked to the teletypes. Hooking his thumbs in his suspenders, he postured at the window. Carol spoke with pride in her voice: "That is noted commentator John W. Vandercook."

I looked at my father. "Who?" I whispered.

Dad bent down. "I've heard him," he said. Although Mr. Vandercook never came in to my bedroom radio, I was impressed to see the man.

Down one more elevator and along yet another hall, Carol halted at a black plastic silhouette of the United States that reached from floor to ceiling. The states were outlined in gold and tiny yellow bulbs blinked on and off under the names of cities labeled in white.

"Those lights indicate a radio station affiliated with the NBC network," Carol said. "See if you can locate the one closest to where you live."

The out-of-towners scanned the silhouette, but I already knew the NBC station closest to Ridgewood. It was WEAF – "Water, Earth, Air and Fire" – in New York City.

Finally, the tour ended where it began, on the mezzanine.

"Thank you for visiting with us today," Carol said. "On behalf of the National Broadcasting Company, I hope you enjoyed our tour, and that you'll come back again."

When she walked away, I made a move to go with her, but Mom and Dad grabbed both my hands and the three of us walked to a desk where a page, brushing specks off his light blue uniform, greeted us.

"Hi, folks. I have free tickets here for today's broadcasts in Radio City."

He pointed to a board on the desk that listed the shows.

"Which would you like to see?"

"Can we go to one, Dad?" I said. He nodded and my mother looked at the list of shows.

"That one!" she said.

The page handed my father three tickets to a variety show in a studio several floors above us. Mom chose it because she liked the host who did another program by himself. Before midnight, Ted Malone read poetry in a soothing voice as an organ played softly behind him.

"I have such a wonderful picture in my mind of how handsome Ted Malone is," Mom said. "I'm thrilled I'm going to see him." *I am, too.*

We were first in line at a red velvet rope stretched between silver poles on the mezzanine. I had to share the broadcast with other adults and kids who fell in behind us, but I didn't mind. *I'm going to see a live radio program with music and laughter and applause.* I hopped on one foot and then the other until a page in a blue uniform appeared.

He escorted us to an elevator, took us to the fifth floor and led us down a hall.

There must be a hundred halls in Radio City! Catching up to the page, I walked in lock-step with him until we reached a large solid door. Pushing it open, he motioned to me to enter.

The studio was smaller than the movie theater at home and much smaller than Studio 8H. My parents chose to sit in a row close to the stage. As soon as I took my seat, I stood back up to look around and my seat flipped up like the ones did at the Warner.

The studio walls were covered by thousands of square white tiles with holes punched in them. I remembered what Carol had said about the odd shapes on the walls of 8H. *They have something to do with "as-coos-tics," I think.*

I glanced at microphones hanging from the ceiling. *If I clap or laugh too loud, will they pick up just the noise I make?* Sitting down again, I looked in the control room. A man in a suit leaned over to an engineer and said something and they both laughed.

How great if I could be in there with them. Enthralled with all I was seeing, I squirmed in my seat until Mom pinched my arm.

"If you have to go to the bathroom, you should have gone before we came in," she whispered.

At last, musicians sauntered on stage and tuned up their instruments. An announcer stepped to a microphone, flashed a toothy grin and greeted us.

"Hi, folks, welcome to *The Ted Malone Show*." I looked at Mom and saw she was smiling. The announcer proceeded to tell us how to applaud.

"Don't just slap your hands together like this," he said, imitating a seal flapping its fins. "Do it forcefully and rapidly. Now, let's try it." I clapped enthusiastically with the audience. "Very good, and when you see me do *this* during the broadcast," he said, making a great circular motion with his arm, "let's really hear it!"

He calmed down and introduced the girl singer and members of the band, and we practiced our clapping as he announced each name.

"We're going on the air in a few moments now, so I'd like to bring out the star of the show." He raised both arms and yelled: "Here's Ted Malone!"

From a door by the control room, a short, bald man with a bushy moustache appeared. He glanced at the audience, his eyes large behind thick lenses of horn-rimmed glasses. As he bounced across the stage, his belly shook. I turned to look at my mother and her hand was up to her mouth. Later, over pie in a restaurant beneath Radio City, Dad and I couldn't resist teasing her.

One of the things I remember most about the Malone program was a solo the pretty girl singer had performed – *Smoke Gets in Your Eyes*. To this day, whenever I hear that tune, I think of the tour, that broadcast and my mother.

MY LOSS

On a crisp September afternoon in 1948, my brother and I were tossing a football on the front lawn when Tom went in the house for a drink of water. He came running out, dragged me by the arm across the street, deposited me on the Eagleson's screened porch and ran back home. Sitting like a lump on a cushioned lounge chair, I didn't say a word to Jean or her mother, but I knew something bad had happened.

By the time Mrs. Eagleson took me over to our house, cars were lined up and down Albert Place and I recognized the black one of our family doctor. My father's Packard was parked in the driveway, so I knew he was home. He stood with solemn-faced neighbors gathered together in the kitchen.

"Hi, Dad," I said in a pinched voice. He didn't respond.

Doctor Esatea sat me down at the cold metal kitchen table.

"Your mother just stopped breathing," he told me.

She was forty-three and had died of a heart attack while fixing dinner. I was twelve and had just started seventh grade. I lowered my head, but didn't cry.

My mother had been laid on my parents' bed in their room down the hall. The doctor looked over at Mrs. Arthur,

Mom's best friend. "We want to take the children in the living room," he said. "Would you close the door to the bedroom?"

"I can't," she replied softly, her eyes down. "Have someone else do it."

The next morning, Grandma Curtis arrived from Union City, and took charge. All day the telephone rang, and people arrived at the door with food. While she and Dad made arrangements, I stayed upstairs.

For two days, I didn't listen to my radio or look at comic books. I wandered into the unfinished portion of the attic, but didn't touch the record player that sat in the hole of the easel. No familiar odors of cooking came up the stairs from the kitchen. Tom stayed in the bedroom, too, and told me what had happened.

"I found Mom slumped on the garbage can by the refrigerator. I ran next door, and Mrs. Van Delden called the doctor."

I knew my mother had died – of that I was certain – but my mind was mixed up with other thoughts. *Because I was born five years after Tom, was I a "surprise" to my parents? Did my birth weaken my mother's heart? Was I to blame for Mom's death?* Because of these questions, I shut down.

At dinner that night, my father didn't sit with Tom and me to talk about what happened. I was quiet and only picked at a neighbor's casserole. On the third day, Grandma Curtis yelled upstairs to get dressed for the funeral.

* * *

That morning, the family drove to C.C. Van Emberg's Funeral Home, a white building with black shutters in downtown Ridgewood. At the black double doors on the side, a long black hearse was parked on a wide black driveway. I looked across the street at the bright windows of

Irving's Drugs and wished I were there, seated at the soda fountain, having a milk shake.

When we entered the carpeted chapel, I was greeted by the soft sound of violins. My father, brother and Grandmother walked down the aisle, and I trailed behind. As I got closer to flowers in vases and wire racks, their smell invaded my nose – a sickening smell.

Sitting on a velvet pew in the front row, I gazed at the casket in front of me. The lid was open and I could see the profile of a face. My mother's face.

One of the funeral employees, a man who lived down the street from us, leaned over to Dad.

"I couldn't prepare Dot," he said of my mother. "I had someone else do it."

People arrived and whispering began. I didn't turn to see who was behind us, but I was sure Aunt Adeline and Uncle Joe had come from Union City. There had to be neighbors from Albert Place, too, as well as parents from school and folks from church.

Relatives from Mom's side of the family are probably not here. My parents talked to Tom and me often about their courtship. Mom's mother and father had felt she married beneath her when she married Dad, a "mere bookkeeper" during the Depression. Even though Dad succeeded with both work and family, that notion persisted through the years with her judgmental brothers and sisters.

I watched as Dr. Platt from the First Presbyterian Church walked to the front of the chapel. My folks insisted I attend Sunday school at his church, but for special services, they let me sit with them in the sanctuary. What he said at the casket was just a jumble of words to me.

When the minister finished speaking, everyone stood up. With my head down, I followed Dad, Tom and Grandma Curtis, walked back up the aisle and left the chapel. A long black Cadillac idled softly behind the hearse outside. We climbed in and rode to the cemetery. No one said a word.

Turning in to George Washington Memorial Park in Paramus, the Cadillac wound past a stand of weeping willows and stopped on a hill. No headstones were in the park: only iron markers flush with the ground identified the graves. We waited while the casket was lifted from the hearse then followed Mom across the grass.

At one side of a four-pole tent, a blue tarp was stretched over a pile of dirt to hide it, but I knew where the dirt had come from. Inside the tent, folding chairs were arranged around the casket now covered by flowers. When I sat, my chair shifted on the bumpy grass.

Dr. Platt walked into the tent and opened his Bible. After he read from it, everyone bowed their heads. The funeral man, the one from our street, came over to my brother and me and took us gently by the elbows.

"You don't need to see the rest," he said and he walked us back to the Cadillac.

Later at home, I stood in the hall outside my parents' bedroom and saw my father crying on my grandmother's shoulder.

"What am I going to do?" he sobbed.

I still didn't cry.

* * *

Neighbors brought more food to the door, and sympathy cards arrived in the mail-box. One afternoon, Mrs. Arthur came across the street to see how Tom and I were doing.

"I need an apron for the boys' cooking class at school," I told her, and she sewed one for me.

Not long after, my father hired a housekeeper, a slow-moving older woman with droopy eyes. Even though she was making beds and preparing dinner when I arrived home from school, the house felt cold and empty. There was no one there to tell about my new friends and school subjects at the junior high.

On weekends, Dad, Tom and I were on our own. We cooked hamburgers in the kitchen Sunday evening while listening to Jack Benny on Mom's radio.

* * *

I began wetting the bed. Twelve years old and I was wetting the bed. After the housekeeper told my father, he took me to see a doctor – not the family's Dr. Esatea, but a special one. The older man sat me on a soft couch surrounded by potted plants in a dimly lit office. He leaned forward in a big leather chair, put his elbows on his knees and talked in a quiet voice.

"Tell me about your school."

"I have subjects in different classrooms," I said. "There's geography, and then I go to science. In cooking class, I got to make meatloaf."

"What do you like to do on Saturday?"

"Ride my bike and go to the movies."

The man had me describe our house. I mentioned the chubby radio in my bedroom.

"What programs do you like?"

"On Monday, *Lux Radio Theater*, but I fall asleep before it's over."

He smiled and asked about my family. I told him about Dad, my brother and Mom. He ended the conversation with a final question.

"Would you like to cry for me now?" The way he said it seemed strange.

Embarrassed, I thought about it for a moment. "No," I answered.

* * *

Through Slanted Windows

Sunday evenings were special if my father took Tom and me to eat at Tony's Restaurant in Hawthorne. We sat on wire-back chairs at a table covered with a red and white checkered cloth speckled with grated cheese from previous customers. Maria, the waitress, snapped her gum as she took Dad's order, then turned and yelled through an open window at Tony in the kitchen. The aroma of tomatoes and meat sauce cooking wafted out every time she went in and out of the kitchen's swinging doors. A plate arrived in front of me piled with Tony's famous ravioli.

A television set, a big black metal box, sat on a shelf that hung from chains hooked in the ceiling. I was happy if we arrived at Tony's in time to see Nazi warships blow up on *Victory at Sea*. The screen was high enough to be seen by patrons in the bar, and I heard them slam down mugs of beer and guffaw when singers and dancers struggled on *Ted Mack's Original Amateur Hour*. The meal at the restaurant was the best one of the week and I would eat Tony's ravioli with gusto.

My father wasn't pleased with the housekeeper, and she was soon dismissed. A neighbor on Albert Place introduced Dad to a younger woman from the Dutch community in Midland Park, New Jersey. At twenty-six, Marge Hazen was a cheerful woman with a ready laugh and soon became a welcome addition to our home.

She did expect more from us in the way of chores, though. My mother had taught me to put clothes out on a school night, but Marge insisted I throw the dirty ones in the hamper, not on the floor, and that Tom and I wipe the kitchen counter after packing our lunches, and oh yes, keep the bathroom at least halfway presentable. I liked her and was happy to discover she listened to the radio as she worked through the house. But she wasn't my Mom.

BEN FRANKLIN

How intimidating Benjamin Franklin Junior High School was when I returned after my mother's funeral. I had been there less than a week when Mom died, and the environment was different than the old stone building on Kenilworth Avenue.

The three-story wing for the seventh, eighth and ninth grades connected to the north end of Ridgewood Senior High to form a red-bricked "T." A bell tower rose above the high school and a terraced lawn with elm trees sloped down to the brick stands at the football field. The whole place looked like a college.

Inside the junior high building, things were not as welcoming. The smell of disinfectant from the custodian's mop lingered in the halls, and the concrete stairs and steel railings were hard and cold. Doors of dark green metal lockers banged one after another when students slammed them shut at the beginning of the day.

I'd never used a locker before, but my home room teacher handed me a card with the number and combination for it. After home room period ended, I hurried to find it, expecting it to be open. However, a black dial with white numbers stuck out above the handle of a narrow closed door.

Looking at the combination on the card, I spun the dial. I tried to lift the handle, but it wouldn't budge. Other students were rushing to first-period classes and the hall was almost empty. Time was running out. *I don't want everyone to look at me if I come in late to class.* I dialed again, careful to land precisely on each number. Lifting the handle, the door wobbled open. *This isn't at all like the simple coat hooks in the cloak rooms at Kenilworth.* I ran into the room for geography as the first bell rang.

The desk I chose had a hard, flat seat attached by a steel brace, but unlike the desks at Kenilworth Elementary, the top was smooth and devoid of ink stains and carvings. A wide canvas roll was above the green chalk board, and when the teacher yanked it down to expose a map, it made a loud, fluttering noise I didn't expect. And I jumped when a speaker crackled alive with a woman's voice summoning someone to the office. Later, a jarring buzzer signaled the end of the period. Gathering up my books, I shoved my way through crowds in the hall to get to my next subject.

It was a comfort to see friends from Kenilworth peppered throughout the classes.

Eventually, I got used to moving every fifty minutes from one classroom to another, and after memorizing the combination to the locker, I spun the dial with confidence. I made new friends by sitting next to kids who fed in from Harrison Avenue and Union Street, the other elementary schools that fed into Ben Franklin.

One afternoon after school, I was alone in the hall with Lester Springstead from Harrison.

"Did your mother really die?" he asked.

His question startled me, and I didn't know how to answer him. *If I say "yes," do I have to give details or should I keep the ordeal to myself?* "What?" was all I could think to say.

"Ah, I'll see you tomorrow," Lester said, and he turned and ran down the stairs.

Over time, I allowed some of my feelings out, though a part of me remained closed inside. This enabled me to get on with my young life, at least on the surface.

* * *

On Friday nights, kids from junior high congregated in the Teen Canteen – a game room in the basement of the First Presbyterian Church. I'd join a group of guys and slouch against a wall trying to act casual. We had crew cuts and wore identical white t-shirts, chinos and brown loafers. On the opposite wall, girls gathered and giggled. They had their hair pulled back in ponytails and wore poodle skirts, bright colored sweaters and brown-and-white saddle shoes. We all sipped bottles of Coca Cola and stole glances at each other.

A pool table sat under bright ceiling lights. The ninth-grade boys dominated the action, so I didn't dare butt in to play. Instead, I ambled over to a card table, grabbed a handful of potato chips from a bowl and stuffed them in my mouth, careful not to drop any on my shirt. I took a gulp of soda from my bottle of Coca Cola, and fizz backed up in my mouth. *I hope it doesn't run out my nose,* I thought in a brief moment of panic.

Looking over the shoulder of Betty Warren at the next table, I watched her struggle to play Canasta with three other girls. She muttered something and threw down her hand of cards. *Did she just say a bad word?*

Moving to another table, I saw four kids hunched over a game of Monopoly.

It was Chucky Hall's turn to roll the dice, but when he tossed them, they bounced off the board, landed at my feet and disappeared.

"Sorry, Chucky. I don't see where they went."

When I saw two stone-faced adults recruited by Dr. Platt to spy on us, I stopped at a safe distance. The man and woman stood with their backs against a wall and surveyed the Teen Canteen with narrow eyes. They saw me, but said nothing.

Through the hubbub of voices, I heard Frankie Laine singing "That's My Desire." Following his voice to an open door, I peered into a darkened room. Girls were in there.

A small table lamp was on in the corner, but someone had draped a scarf over the shade to soften the light. Next to the lamp was a small phonograph that played 45s. The song ended and I put my Coke bottle down and entered the room. Walking over to a girl – I wasn't certain who she was because of the dim light – I was happy to discover Gail Kent.

"Would you like to dance?" I asked, hoping my voice wouldn't crack. She rose and gave me her hand as Joni James began to sing "Why Don't You Believe Me?"

Gail's hand was warm in mine. I touched her waist as she rested her other hand on my shoulder. We maneuvered the boxy steps of the Fox Trot we both learned in elementary school. She was softer and smelled better than any boy I ever wrestled with in the grass. It was then that I made up my mind to return to the Teen Canteen every Friday night and expand my circle of friends to the cute ones with the curves.

JERRY AND UNCLE MILTIE

Jerry Wells and I walked home together often from Ben Franklin. At Spring Avenue, he'd peel off to his parent's big house with the two car garage at the end of the street and I'd continue on to the little home on Albert Place in the subdivision. One afternoon, he invited me to his home.

The basement in the Wells' house was finished in real knotty pine paneling and a red linoleum tile floor. I was impressed that the paneling and tile even went into the laundry room and workshop. An upright piano stood at the foot of the stairs. Jerry took lessons on it and was a pretty good player. We sat side-by-side on the bench and sang songs from sheet music propped above the keys. Mrs. Wells listened at the open door upstairs.

We started with a song by Julie London, but didn't sound at all like the sultry singer when we told Mrs. Wells to "Cry Me A River."

On the next one, I added sound effects to make our rendition different than Nat "King" Cole's.

"Crash, bam, (Two shakes of the shade on a floor lamp) alakazam."

Mrs. Wells yelled down.

"Leave the lamp alone."

Jerry flipped over the sheet music and Bing Crosby's photo appeared on a cover. Our serenade continued without attempting to croon like him on "Poor Little Lambs." We sang the "baaa baaa" part pretty good however.

In spite of our less-than-stellar singing, the door to the basement remained open, but when Jerry heard Mrs. Wells close the kitchen door and go outside to water her flowers, he ran upstairs. Coming back, he had his father's dictation machine clutched in his hands. Setting the squat device on top of the piano, he plugged it in and dangled a small round microphone over the keys. After he turned it on, we proceeded to sing and talk onto the spinning spool of wire of the machine.

We performed our limited repertoire of songs – interspersed with witty dialogue, of course – and then Jerry rewound the wire. He pushed a button and the tinny sound of our voices came out of the machine's nickel-sized speaker. It was the first time I heard my own voice.

Why don't I sound like the announcers I hear on the networks? I sound like a kid.

We listened until a thought occurred to me.

"Jerry! What if we recorded over some dictation of your father's?"

We laughed picturing the reaction of his dad's secretary when she heard two kids singing in her ear piece. Then Jerry's face fell. He probably realized what would happen when his father found we had recorded over some important dictation. Jerry quickly wound up the microphone cord, unplugged the machine and ran it back upstairs. I was sorry he did. I wanted to hear my voice on the wire again.

* * *

There was a television set in the rumpus room of the Wells' basement. It was the first one in the neighborhood. From the back of the wooden cabinet, a flat brown wire ran up a wall, disappeared in the ceiling and connected to an antenna lashed onto the chimney. When a plastic knob was pulled, a ten-inch screen flickered and a black-and-white picture took form. By clicking a larger knob, Jerry showed me the seven stations the set could bring in from Channel 2 all the way around to Channel 13. Even though Jerry and I were sophisticated junior high kids, we watched *Howdy Doody Time* after school hoping Buffalo Bob would show an old time silent movie.

Tuesdays, Mrs. Wells set up the room like a theater. She turned stuffed chairs and a couch toward the TV, pulled metal folding chairs out of a closet, dragged the bench over from the piano and brought a chair with a pillow tied on the seat from her sewing room. At eight p.m., neighbors from blocks around tromped down the stairs.

My brother and I sat in the front row and watched as four men dressed as gas station attendants appeared on the screen. They stood shoulder to shoulder and sang.

"Oh, we're the men of Tex-a-co, we work from Maine to Mex-i-co, there's nothing like this Texaco of ooouuurrrs." Ending the song, they shouted in unison.

"And now, the star of the show... Milton... Berle!"

As an audience burst into applause, a man in a suit ran in front of the singers. He put two fingers in his mouth and whistled, motioned for the clapping to continue, kicked up a leg and yelled: "Wee Wee! Wow Wow!"

For the next hour, Milton Berle cavorted with high energy and told corny jokes stolen from other comedians for which he was dubbed "The Thief of Bad Gags."

In one skit, Berle came out wearing an evening gown and a braided blonde wig.

With his mouth smeared with lipstick, he flirted at the camera, blinking long fake eye lashes. I felt uneasy seeing a man dressed like a woman.

He turned out feet in high heels and stomped around on the sides of the shoes until a skinny little man ran out, yelled

"Make-up!" and smacked Berle in the face with a sock full of flour. The people in the Wells' basement roared with laughter along with the audience of *The Texaco Star Theater*.

In spite of his outrageous antics, Berle was welcomed into millions of homes in America every Tuesday night. He became our "Uncle Miltie."

The next morning, Jerry and I marched side by side down the hall at Ben Franklin and sang the gas station attendants' song from Berle's show. We sang as much as we had learned then mumbled about pumping the gas, rubbing the hubs and cleaning the glass. At the door of our home room, we stopped, got down on one knee and finished big to the delight of our classmates.

"We're the merry Tex-a-co-men. Tonight we may be show-men. Tomorrow we'll be ser-vic-ing your caaar."

DAD'S CITY

With Mom gone, my father wanted to do something special with his two sons. One Saturday morning in winter, Tom and I piled in the Packard and Dad drove us into Manhattan.

The first stop was at a three story building on upper Broadway, the New York office for the Packard Motor Car Company. At the entrance on the side to the parking garage, an elderly Negro attendant rose from his stool.

"Good morning, Mister Archard," the man called out.

Rolling down his window, Dad said "Good morning, Bill. Where have you been?"

"On vacation," the man answered.

"Well, it looks like you got a good tan," Dad said.

Both men laughed as my father pulled ahead to his parking space. At the time, the brief repartee seemed funny and I thought nothing of it.

We went upstairs to a row of offices along a balcony. Leaning over the railing, Tom and I marveled at the shiny Packard's on the showroom floor below. A salesman sat reading a newspaper, and another held the door open for a couple entering from Broadway. The lady wore a fur around her neck, and the man carried a walking stick. *I hope they'll buy a Packard for Dad's sake.*

When my father introduced us to the office people who came into work that morning, a portly man with garters on his sleeves squeezed my brother's arm.

"My, what a tall boy you are, Tom," he said.

A woman with glasses pushed up the hair on her head stepped forward.

"This must be David," she said, tousling my hair.

Their voices sounded overly cheerful and their smiles were forced. *Are they actually sad to meet the motherless boys from New Jersey?*

We followed my father into his office. While he busied himself with papers on his desk, I swiveled on a chair with wheels and Tom picked up a telephone. Dad growled: "Put the phone down before the operator comes on."

After I used the men's room further along the balcony, we said goodbye to the office people. As we went down the stairs, I looked back and saw a secretary dab at her eyes with a hankie. Our depleted family stepped out on Broadway and took a cab to Times Square.

Arriving at a restaurant with lace curtains in two small windows, we were met by a short man in a black suit at the door. In a strong Italian accent, he greeted my father by name and asked us to follow him.

We were led to a table covered with white cloth, shiny silverware and napkins stuffed through gold rings. When a waiter in a stiff shirt and bow tie approached, I knew this was not the place to order a hamburger. Dad picked out lunch for the three of us from a menu so big it covered his face when he held it up to read. While we ate, Tom and I chattered away about the Packard's we had seen that morning and which ones we liked best.

Leaving the restaurant, we fell in with a crowd rushing by. Steam spewing from manhole covers had melted the snow, and gray puddles of slush lay in the gutters. We side-stepped smelly garbage cans stuffed with bulging bags. Although my legs were strong from bike riding, I had trouble keeping up with the long strides of my father especially on such busy sidewalks. Before I had a chance to ask him to slow down, Dad stopped under a marquee with a hundred blinking lights. He spoke to the pretty girl in a booth.

"One adult and two children."

He slid money through an opening in her glass window, she slid out three tickets and we entered the Roxy Theater.

The lobby was as big as the football field at Ridgewood High School, and way above over our heads, a row of chandeliers glistened. Dad's shoes clicked on the marble floor as we hurried to a flight of thick carpeted stairs.

The theater's auditorium had velvet seats I had to push down like the ones at the Warner back home. Although the size of the auditorium reminded me of big Studio 8H at Radio City, the Roxy had rows of thick columns holding up the roof. I stared at a tan curtain stretching across the giant stage and followed its pleats up a hundred feet to a galaxy of stars splashed on the ceiling. By twisting my neck, I watched them blink all the way back to the open windows of the projection room.

Before long, the lights in the theater went off and the curtain parted. A screen, twice as big as the Warner's, came alive with the shaggy head of the MGM lion. I settled back in my seat because I knew an action story or musical always followed his roar.

A Technicolor movie began, and as the music played, the stars' names appeared.

Fred Astaire! I wish I could dance like he does with Ginger Rogers.

Red Skelton! I can imitate the characters he does on his radio program.

Astaire and Skelton played songwriters in a place called "Tin Pan Alley." I sang along in my head with the title song, "Three Little Words," whenever it came on in the movie.

When the movie ended, the curtain closed and a spotlight in the balcony threw a circle of light on the pleats. I was amazed to see a microphone on a stand rise from the floor of the stage. *What's going to happen next?* A voice boomed overhead: "Ladies and gentlemen, please welcome Bud Abbott and Lou Costello!"

The audience whistled and applauded as two men ran out on the stage into the circle of light. I sat on the edge of my seat, excited that I was seeing the pair I heard on the radio and saw at the movies.

Abbott, tall and slim, wore a fedora hat like my father's and started firing questions at his partner. Costello, short and round with a small pork pie hat perched on his head, answered with funny faces and poses.

When Abbott got angry at Costello's antics, he pummeled the little guy with his fists. Costello pulled his hat down over his ears and cried like a baby. I laughed as hard as the rest of the audience.

At the close of their act, Abbott described a baseball game to Costello. He announced the players and their positions by naming them "Who," "What" and "Ida Know" to confuse Costello.

"Who's on first," Abbott began. "What's on second and Ida Know is on third."

"Wait a minute, wait a minute," said Costello. "Give me those names again. Who's on first?"

"Yes." Abbott replied.

"What's his name?" said Costello.

"Who," said Abbott.

"The guy on first!" Costello screamed.

He became frustrated and jammed his hat down on his head.

"Okay. What's on second?" he said.

"That's right," said Abbott.

"I wanna know which player is on second."

"What."

The short man got red in the face and spun around.
"Alright, who's playing third?" he said.
"No, Who's playing first."
"I said which man is playing third base?"
"Ida Know."

Costello jumped up and down and it looked like steam would come out of his ears. The audience howled. It was good to hear my Dad laugh.

AIRWAVES AT NIGHT

Sam Drapkin and his brothers, three little old men in gray smocks, scurried around the candy counters and magazine racks of their store in downtown Ridgewood.

Drapkin's was long and narrow with a door and two windows facing the street. Past the tobacco and out-of-town newspapers, the store opened up in the back to floor-to-ceiling shelves loaded with toys.

One year, under the watchful eye of my mother, I had spent birthday money there. Dawdling at the shelves, I agonized over choosing a Tootsie Toy from everyone ever made. There were airplanes, too, and Lincoln Logs and American Bricks and chemistry sets, board games, picture puzzles, stuffed animals and books. At Mom's urging, I made a decision and ran up the aisle of the store clutching a truck hauler filled with little metal cars on real rubber wheels.

"Stop at the cash register," she called out. "You have to pay for that."

I couldn't wait to get home and play with my new treasure.

Of course, as a fourteen year old in 1950, I had stopped going to the toys in the back and instead scanned the magazine racks in front. After the movies one Saturday, I stood chewing a Y and S licorice whip and looked up and down at the bright covers. The word "radio" jumped out at me from a simple pulp paper booklet. Pulling it out, I was amazed at what I held in my hand.

White's Radio Log listed all the radio stations in the U.S.A., every one of them, in all the forty-eight states! I dug in my pocket, hoping I'd have enough coins left from the movies. I paid one of the little Drapkin brothers and ran to the bus station. Settling in to a big leather seat on the orange and brown bus, I buried my nose in the booklet.

The first pages of *White's Radio Log* had stations listed alphabetically by call letters, the ones west of the Mississippi River that began with K followed by the ones that started with W in the part of the country where I lived.

I looked up WPAT right away. My finger went down the columns. *WP, WPA, there it is! WPAT, Paterson, N.J.* The booklet had its facts straight.

Stations were listed next by frequency, 540 all the way to 1600 kilocycles. *Let's see if WPAT is listed under 930. It is!* The booklet was accurate.

Absorbed in the booklet as the bus chugged along, I almost missed my stop. Glancing out the window, I saw Albert Place a block away and yanked the cord. The rest of the day was spent at home pouring over the new treasure from Drapkin's.

In time, I memorized almost every station in *White's Radio Log,* and could challenge people on this subject. I'd ask them to toss out the name of a city in the K or W part of the country, then bet them I could tell at least one radio station licensed to it.

"Phoenix."
"KOY!"
"Baltimore."
"WITH!"
"Louisville."

"WHAS!"
I became a whiz kid with a head full of call letters.

* * *

When the sun went down and the clouds were just right, I discovered I could pick up other stations on my bedroom radio besides ones from New York and surrounding areas. *White's Radio Log* helped me find the stations on the dial that threw powerful signals into the night sky from huge 50,000-watt transmitters in cities far away.

The first night I began my search, I stretched out on the bed and placed the radio on my stomach. *I'll try to pull in WCAU from Philadelphia. That's just done from New Jersey, and over in the next state. White's Radio Log* told me the station was at 1210 kilocycles. When I set the dial to where I thought the frequency was, a jumble of voices and music talked and played on top of one another until a network program I recognized broke through the noise. The log indicated that WCAU was a CBS affiliate, so I hung on, hoping the signal wouldn't fade as call letters would be given after the program. At last, a man said "This is WCAU, 1210 in Philadelphia" before the station shrunk back into the hubbub. *That's one. What else?*

I moved the needle slightly to the right of 1500, and the deep voice of "John R" came in, introducing a rhythm and blues record on WLAC, 1510 in Nashville. It sounded as loud as WPAT in nearby Paterson, but after a few minutes, the station and Mr. "R" left me. Turning the dial back the other way, I set the needle carefully to the right of WOR.

To my surprise, the snippet of a Cubs game came in at 720 from WGN, Chicago until the game and station faded into the night. It was a joy when I touched the waxed wire backing of the radio with my left hand while dialing with my right. My body became an antennae and more stations could be brought in if only for a few precious moments. How exciting it was to lie under the eaves of a house in Ridgewood, New Jersey, and hear stations from cities thousands of miles away.

* * *

One night I hurried through dinner and homework because a network radio program was going to originate from Ridgewood. *America's Town Meeting of the Air* was going on at eight p.m. from the YMCA, and I wanted to see it. Riding the orange and brown bus downtown seemed to take forever.

When I arrived at the auditorium on the second floor of the Y, a man was unlatching a black metal trunk with letters A B C stenciled on the side. I figured he was an engineer from the network in New York. *He must have dragged the trunk up the stairs by himself.*

I watched closely as he placed three microphones with desk stands on a long table in the front the auditorium stage and twisted a fourth microphone onto a floor stand.

Using both hands, he lifted a metal box from the trunk with knobs, switches, a meter on the front and a long cord with a plug dangling from the back. Plugging it in to a nearby wall socket, the meter lit up and glowed yellow. Next, he unraveled a thin wire from the box and used a screwdriver to attach it to a connection on the wall's baseboard.

Remembering what my hard-cover radio book taught me about remote broadcasts, I knew the engineer had hooked up the box to a telephone line to the network in New York. After he pushed the microphone cords into sockets on the back of the box, he sat down and lit a cigarette.

People came in to the auditorium and sat on metal folding chairs arranged theater-style. There were students as well as adults, but I didn't see any of my own classmates in the crowd. The panelists and moderator entered and took their places at the long table.

A tall, distinguished man with gray hair strode to the mike on the floor stand and glanced at the round-faced clock by the engineer's chair. *That's gotta be the announcer.*

"We're going on the air in a few moments," he said in a deep, mellow voice and told the audience to applaud on his signal. He then said the subject for the evening's broadcast would be the continuation of U.S. foreign aid going to the Asian country of Vietnam.

"If you have a question or comment for the panel, raise your hand and I'll escort you to this microphone," he instructed. Apparently the program wanted to get the thoughts from citizens of Ridgewood, but being fourteen in 1950, I had nothing to offer to the upcoming discussion and no way was I going to step to the microphone and croak to the nation.

The announcer stood erect and cleared his throat. The clock's second hand met the minute hand straight up at eight p.m. and the engineer threw him a finger cue.

"From the YMCA in Ridgewood, New Jersey, we bring you this week's 'America's Town Meeting of the Air,'" he intoned. He said it with such confidence that a shiver went up my back. *He was just heard by millions of people across the country, and I'm in the same room with him.* For the next hour, I didn't pay attention to what the panel talked about, but concentrated on the announcer. He listened intently to the discussion, jotted a few words on a clip board and kept looking at the clock. When people raised their hands, he took them by their elbows and led them to the floor mike to speak.

My gaze shifted to the engineer. With earphones clamped on his head, he adjusted the knobs on the box whenever anyone spoke. I kept thinking how everything was going out to hundreds of stations coast to coast. I worried I might sneeze, or the metal folding chair I was sitting on would fold up and crash to the floor. I was almost afraid to breathe.

At the end of the hour, the announcer used a circular motion with his hand to tell the moderator to wind up the discussion. The moderator did, the audience applauded and the announcer approached the floor mike again. Signing off the program, he gave his name: "George Gunn speaking. This is ABC, the America Broadcasting Company."

George Gunn! I know this man! I had heard him on other shows, but didn't recognize his voice.

When everyone stood up to leave, I wanted to go over to him and introduce myself, but didn't. *What professional announcer from New York would want to speak to a skinny kid out in Jersey with a passion to be on the radio?* George Gunn left the auditorium, the engineer put his equipment back in the trunk, and I went home.

* * *

In the mid-fifties, live music was disappearing from the radio as more stations switched over to records. When I got home from school, I would sing along with Perry Como, Theresa Brewer, the Four Lads and other popular singers of the day as Martin Block played their recordings over and over on WNEW's *Make Believe Ballroom*.

While he drove home from work, my father listened to sportscaster-turned-music-announcer Ted Husing on WHN. Dad told me he liked Husing because he included a mix of Dixieland records to his program.

Late on Friday nights, I would tune in Symphony Sid on WJZ. He had replaced the dance band remotes from swanky nightclubs with bebop records played in his booth at *Birdland*, a New York nightspot where the great jazz musicians congregated. I also listened to Freddie Robbins spin jazz records out of his *Robbins Nest* on WOV. Coming across a photo of the baby-faced host in *Downbeat* magazine, I couldn't help wondering how Robbins got into radio at such a young age.

Another issue of *Downbeat* ran a contest to have readers come up with a title for Robbins, Symphony Sid, Husing, Block and all the rest who played records on the radio. Out of the entries submitted – including the rejected "discomboobulator" – the magazine chose "disc jockey." Finally, I knew what I wanted to do in radio. As I had grown up, I was attracted to performers of the times – funny characters on comedy shows and straight-talking announcers on murder mysteries – but when radio changed, I changed, too. *I'm going to be a "disc jockey" and ride platters on the air.*

TOM

A quiet man with rimless glasses came to the house once a week, set up a wire music stand in the living room and gave my brother trumpet lessons. He breezed through the scales in the practice book and soon advanced to playing songs from sheet music.

Before long, the teacher told my father that Tom had the lips, lungs and ear of a gifted musician.

Besides sitting as first chair trumpet in the Ridgewood High School orchestra, Tom led the brass section in the marching band at football games. At half time, he performed on the field in his maroon uniform and tall white hat with the shiny black bill. I'd nudge whoever was next to me in the bleachers, point and say "That's my brother."

* * *

The first time Tom allowed me to follow him into a two-story building across from the A & P in Ridgewood, I felt I was entering his private domain. Most afternoons after school and on Saturday, he could be found inside Agel's Music Store.

He headed to the record bins and I wandered around on the floor. A shiny gold trumpet, black clarinet and silver saxophone were displayed high on a wall. *What's holding them up there?*

I touched the smooth wood of a yellow guitar leaning back on a foot stand and ran my fingers across the strings of its shiny neck. *I bet I could play that.*

Gazing at a rack filled with sheet music of popular songs, I recognized the Andrews Sisters from their movies. Covers on other sheets showed faces of singers I heard only on my radio. *Patti Page is pretty.*

From where I stood, I could hear someone playing scales on a piano in the back of the store. A boy carrying a black instrument case shaped like a trumpet was climbing the staircase for a lesson on the second floor. Music was everywhere. Agel's was a musical candy store for my brother.

Tom motioned me over to the records lined up in wooden bins clear to the back wall. Categories for the thick black discs were printed in bold letters for "New Releases," "Popular," "Jazz," "Show-Broadway," "Country-Western" and "Opera-Classical." Flipping through the ones in the "Popular" bin, I saw which recording companies had produced a song. Through the round openings of green paper sleeves, I read the names : Decca, RCA, Capitol and others. Picking up a record by singer Andy Russell, I turned the disc over and found a second song by him on the other side.

I discovered a flat, heavy cardboard box and lifted it up. I saw a photograph on the cover of a man holding a clarinet in front of a band. The box opened like a book, revealing four discs in brown paper sleeves. Labels on the discs informed me that the songs were recorded by Artie Shaw and his orchestra. All eight selections were being sold together as a package. I was holding a record "album" for the first time.

In one corner of Agel's was a small booth with a window, and inside a young man and a girl were bobbing their heads. I didn't understand why until the door was opened by the girl and the sound of Tommy Dorsey's band flowed out. I peeked in, saw a record spinning on a turntable and realized the booth was where my brother sampled recordings before he bought them.

I followed Tom out of the store knowing that the white Agel's bag under his arm held a new addition to his record collection. At home, he placed a black 78 disc on the mast of his record changer and turned it on.

"Listen to this," he said, and pushed a lever.

The disc slapped down on the turntable and began to spin. The pick-up arm moved in, the needle eased down, and the sound of the trumpet of Harry James came blaring from the speaker.

On other days, I heard trumpet greats like Charlie Shavers, Bix Beiderbecke and Louis Armstrong and soon became a lover of all kinds of jazz from Dixieland to the big band sound. When long-play albums began coming into Agel's with six selections pressed on each side of a thin vinyl platter, Tom was excited. He bought a record player that spun a turntable at the new speed of 33 and 1/3 revolutions per minute, so he could hear trumpet players perform a new kind of jazz. My brother brought home Miles Davis from Agel's one week and Dizzy Gillespie the next. Bebop flooded our bedroom as he played his albums over and over. We both sang with Diz on one selection: "Oop bop sh'bam a klook a mop."

* * *

Before graduating from high school, my brother was awarded a scholarship to the school of music at Syracuse University. After making poor grades, he returned home and enlisted in the Army. Flown to Germany, he was assigned to a military band to greet officials by day and to a dance band to entertain officers at night. His talent with the trumpet was kept from the United States for the next three years.

LEAVING WITH A BANG

William Welch, the science teacher at Benjamin Franklin Junior High School, was a short, balding man who spoke as though his jaws were wired together. When he cracked a weak joke, he'd curl his upper lip and laugh through clenched teeth: "Hee, hee, hee." We called him "Wee Willie" behind his back.

He doubled as our home room teacher. Mornings, a few malcontent boys and a group of girls gathered in his classroom to have attendance taken, say the pledge to the flag and hear announcements. We played a few mild pranks on "Wee Willie," but a big one would come at the end of the school year.

To celebrate our graduation from junior high in the spring of 1951, the ninth-grade class put on a talent show in the high school auditorium. My old friend Jerry Wells, another buddy, Randy Hopper and I asked the teacher in charge if we could do a pantomime to Debbie Reynolds' recording of "Abba Dabba Honeymoon." She said that sounded fine and signed us up. Little did she know what we had in mind to spice up our performance.

Bill Aiken was brighter than he looked for a ninth-grader, but the lumbering kid with the hint of a beard towered over the rest of the boys. Wells, Hopper and I convinced him to join us in our act, and rehearsals began in secret.

On the day of the talent show, our turn to go on began with Debbie Reynolds singing from a record player in the wings about the happy chim-pan-zee in the Congo-land. Jerry, Randy and I ambled out on stage dressed in brown shirts and shorts. Wells wore a pith helmet he'd found in his parent's closet. Hopper clomped along with a walking stick, and I carried two buckets. Slight laughter rippled through the auditorium.

I placed the buckets down and made sure the audience saw that the first one was filled with water. I scooped up some with a cupped hand and let it drip back through my fingers. Randy did the same. Laughter grew as the audience anticipated that something was going to happen with the buckets. Debbie sped up her singing with repeated abba-dabba-dabbas which was Bill Aiken's cue to come swinging out from the wings out on a rope sling. We had smeared his arms, legs and chest with orange makeup and dressed him in a furry vest, shorts and nothing else. The audience howled.

As Debbie went on singing, I ignored the first bucket with the water, but picked up the second one. Jerry, Randy and I ran down the steps of the stage and into the auditorium. The audience screamed.

Before the show, we had told the audio-visual nerd in the balcony to follow us with his spotlight. We stopped in the aisle where Mr. Welch was seated and I handed the bucket to Jerry. The audience shrieked. Wells reared back and launched a pail full of confetti over "Wee Willie." Pandemonium broke out.

Students stood and yelled and whistled. Teachers in the front row turned around and raised their arms for quiet. Mr. Welch sat there grinning as tiny bits of paper fluttered off his head and into his lap. Nobody heard the end of Debbie's song. The laughter and applause lasted a full minute as the three of us scrambled back on stage and disappeared into the wings. Aiken struggled to get his bare foot out of the rope sling as the curtain closed.

The next morning, Principal Geary pulled Jerry, Randy, Bill, and me out of home room. He was livid. We stood nonchalantly in the hall as he used the words "outrageous" and "disrespectful."

"If this wasn't the last week of school, I'd throw you all out. And you," he said, glaring at me. "Stop chewing that gum."

He turned and stomped away.

Back in home room, Mr. Welch smiled.

"Don't worry, boys. I thought it was funny."

SENIOR ACADEME

In the fall of 1951, I swaggered along the halls of Ridgewood High School as a confident tenth-grader. Biology, like English and history, was a required course, so on the first day, I dutifully entered the classroom with the rest of the students. Microscopes were lined up ready for young biologists to inspect amoebas, and weird black and red insects posed on twisted brown and green twigs inside bell jars. On the wall, a shiny poster exposed the intestines of a bloated frog. In front of the room stood Mr. Raffensberger – our short, balding biology teacher – looking at us like a smiling garden gnome as we took our seats.

His first duty was to teach us about the twenty-eight-day menstrual cycle of girls and how it related to reproduction. Bugs and frogs would have to wait. We were going to learn about sex.

Both genders sat rigid and stared straight ahead as Mr. Raffensberger chattered on while fiddling with a white stick of chalk in his hand. Drawing a diagram on the black board that showed tubes filled with circles, he added squiggly lines that looked like tad-poles swimming up to them. Each time he finished explaining something in his diagram, he'd turn around to us and, using two words in one, say "Y'see?"

Mr. Raffensberger finished, his face red. With the reproduction lecture over, we all relaxed and went on to dissecting big grasshoppers.

*   *   *

After selecting my academic subjects, I was given a list of extra-curricular activities to choose from. I was excited to read about something called *Journalism Radio*. *What the heck is that?* Mr. Bowler, my home room teacher, enlightened me. "The Journalism Club gathers school news during the week and delivers it on the public address system at Friday's assemblies," he explained.

"Where do I sign-up?"

At the first meeting after school, I joined a group of seasoned eleventh and twelfth-graders. The older members got cushy assignments to cover the senior class play, the cooking club and the cheerleaders. Being the lone sophomore, I was given the job of reporting on the boys' Saturday basketball league.

The teams practicing in the gym after lunch gave me the opportunity to gather facts for my story. Obeying the rule of the custodians, I took off my shoes at the edge of the court and went on the floor in my socks. Slipping around with a pad and pencil, I ducked passes, dodged elbows and yelled my questions at team captains between balls slamming on backboards: "What team did you play?" "What was the score?" "Who made the most baskets?"

Out of the confusion, I gathered enough answers to put a report together. How accurate my scribbled notes were, I didn't know. I hadn't the sense to sit in the quiet of the Phys. Ed. office and get everything I needed out of the stat book.

At Friday's assembly, a microphone on a stand was placed on the stage, but behind the curtain lest the Journalism Club be seen and the illusion of *Journalism Radio* ruined. Students and teachers arrived, banging down wooden seats in the auditorium, their voices echoing off the high ceiling.

Members of the club sauntered out from the wings with me tripping behind them.

Butterflies fluttered in my stomach that morning and my sandwich bag stayed in the locker at lunch time. When the principal pushed his way through the part in the curtain, I got a glimpse of people in the first row, but recognized no one.

The auditorium fell silent as Dr. Brown began his announcements. Backstage, I rose on my toes, took a deep breath and eased down slowly, letting air out through pursed lips. The principal returned through the curtain, and it was time for *Journalism Radio*.

Reporters stepped up and delivered their stories in strong, confident tones. When my turn came, I advanced to the microphone and stood before it, weak-kneed. The slots of the mike's silver head seemed to grin at me. I looked at the thin wire snaking across the floor that would send my voice out to the multitude in the auditorium. I swallowed and opened my mouth. Air passed through my vocal cords, my lips moved and words came out. It was my report. *I researched it, wrote it and now I'm doing it!* Concentrating on the clarity of delivery, my eyes carefully picked each word off the piece of paper that shook in my hand. In my own ears, my voice sounded thin and high-pitched, just as it had on the dictation machine in Jerry Wells' basement. I reached the end and stepped back, drained.

As a member closed off the edition of *Journalism Radio*, a senior tapped me on the shoulder, motioned for me to follow him, and we hurried off the stage. The curtain opened to reveal the Music Club seated with their instruments poised for a recital, and the audience applauded. *Are they clapping for the musicians or for me and what I've just done?*

* * *

While getting ready for school each morning, I dialed around to sample the wake-up shows on the New York stations. Two of them still featured live music instead of records. WOR's John Gambling – the man who read school closings on snow days – had a trio of musicians who sawed out old tunes on sour-sounding violins. Jack Sterling on WCBS, though, was backed by a pretty good jazz band. If my brother was home, I knew he'd say "Hey, turn that up."

Every morning, Sterling talked to a member in the band named Tyree Glenn. An article in Tom's *Downbeat* told me Glenn was a famous jazz trombonist. I pictured him stumbling into Sterling's studio at dawn after jamming all night at smoky *Birdland*, gulping coffee and playing on the air until nine before going home to bed.

WALLY AND MARY

While dialing on the bedroom radio one Saturday night, I landed on WNBC, and my ears perked up. Two men were doing a parody of the popular radio program, *Mr. Keen, Tracer of Lost Persons* – only they twisted the title to *Mr. Trace, Keener than Most Persons*. The pair did a take-off on a television ad for an automobile, ending it with a tag line from a cigarette commercial that made no sense: "And it's milder. Much milder."

Next, they lampooned a soap opera, the sponsor being "Dirt, the maker of Mud." There was no studio audience, but I heard the band and girl singer laughing. I had discovered Bob and Ray.

According to a newspaper article I read, Bob Elliott and Ray Goulding worked together in the morning on a station in Boston – Bob playing records, and Ray announcing the news. They kidded around on the air, and their give-and-take developed into funny routines that featured offbeat characters portrayed by their two voices. Soon, records and news became secondary to their comedy. NBC heard them, brought them to New York and put them on the radio network.

I laughed out loud at the bits and skits Bob and Ray wrote or ad-libbed. A spoof of the soap opera *Mary Nobel, Backstage Wife* was named *Mary Backstage, Noble Wife*. They'd do an interview in which the guest lent nothing to the subject, had no idea why he was doing it, got mad and left. Much of their comedy was satire that could be understood only by listeners whose knowledge of the broadcasting industry gave them a frame of reference. As a radio aficionado at age fifteen, I caught on to Bob and Ray right away.

In the cafeteria at Ridgewood High, I introduced my buddies to the names and voices created by the pair. I imitated Bob as reporter Wally Ballew with the stopped-up nose. They cracked up when I made my voice go falsetto like Ray's did when he became lovable Mary McGoon. Her down east New England reply to a question soon became a catch phrase at school: "A-ya, surely."

It was difficult to follow Bob and Ray around on WNBC. After the funny Saturday night show, network geniuses kept trying them at different times on different days. I was shocked to read in the Sunday *Radio Guide* that they'd been assigned to host a quiz show called *Pick and Play with Bob and Ray*. It was though NBC didn't know what to do with the talented pair.

* * *

On a spring afternoon, my high school buddies and I were draped over living room furniture in the home of Sam Hayes. The five of us were sulking because some friends had gone to Florida on Easter break and we were jealous. Sam's mother put up with our droopy faces for just so long.

"Oh, for Gawd's sake," she exclaimed in her sweet Carolina accent. "Why don't y'all go into the city for a day or two? Visit the zoo. See a show. It'll be my treat."

The next morning, Bill Dailey, Jerry Van Riper, Halsey Sheffield, Sam and I woke up in the Hotel Taft with a whole day in Manhattan ahead of us. Getting dressed, I convinced the guys we should go to Radio City and hang around.

"They do the *Today* show on TV right off the street," I said. "People stand at the window and hold up signs saying 'Hi Mom in Omaha.' When it's over, we can go in and look around. It's something we gotta do!"

Long after *Today* had signed off, we arrived at the studio on West 49th Street. No one was in the place. Overhead lights were off, teletype machines were silent and cameras were tilted down with caps on their lenses.

We wandered around the carpeted set and inspected the S-shaped blue desk surrounded by soft chairs on wheels. I sat where Dave Garroway did to host the program. Looking at a TV screen built flush with the desk top, I imagined I was he, talking with reporters from all over the country.

Out on the sidewalk, I impressed my buddies with knowledge of Garroway.

"He was a low-key disc jockey at midnight on WMAQ in Chicago," I told them. "I watched a Sunday TV show he did from there. To end it one evening, he whacked the cable to New York with a hatchet and the screen went dark." We stepped off the curb and dashed across 49th Street. *Will I be a low-key disc jockey when I get on the air?*

We entered the RCA Building under the gray and silver overhang with the red neon words "NBC STUDIOS." Remembering the tour when I was a kid, I marched up the carpeted stairs to the network. My buddies tagged along behind me wondering where the heck I was going. The desk was still on the mezzanine, staffed with a page in a blue uniform offering free tickets for the day's broadcasts from Radio City. I spotted tickets with incredible words: "The Colgate Palmolive Peet Company presents the Bob and Ray Show."

Through Slanted Windows

"Those!" I said.

The page told us when to return and we ran back down to the street floor with me grasping five tickets. The guys were excited about seeing the pair they heard so much about from me.

"I want to find a pay phone and call my mother," Sam said, "and tell her we're going to see a live radio show." My mind flashed on my mom and the broadcast we saw together with Dad in the same building. With time to kill, we decided to walk around Rockefeller Center, but before leaving the RCA Building, I told my buddies to go ahead of me.

"I'll wait here for a moment then come out with my dark glasses on. You guys rush up to me like I'm a celebrity and ask for my autograph."

After they left, I counted slowly to ten and made a grand exit onto 49th Street. My friends were nowhere in sight. I found them around the corner, laughing. "Very funny," I grumbled.

At the appointed time for the broadcast, we returned to NBC and fell in line with a crowd on the mezzanine. A page appeared and escorted us to a studio on the sixth floor. *Could we be going to the same one I was in with Mom and Dad to see Ted Malone?* When we entered, a puny band of four musicians were tuning up their instruments on a cramped stage. A sound effects man and his equipment occupied limited space in back of them. Metal folding chairs were arranged on the flat floor for the audience. "Couldn't NBC have given Bob and Ray Studio 8H with its plush seats?" I asked under my breath.

A smiley announcer stepped to a microphone.

"Hi, folks, I'm Glenn Riggs. In a few moments, you're going to see a live fifteen-minute program on the NBC network for Colgate, starring the great comedy team of Bob Elliott and Ray Goulding. And please stay in your seats at the end of the program because right afterward we'll be taping *another* Bob and Ray show that'll be played on the air tomorrow." I leaned over to my buddies. "Wow, two shows for one ticket!"

Glenn Riggs told us when to applaud on his signal. "And be sure to laugh if you want to," he added with a bigger smile.

Glancing at the clock above the slanted control room window, he introduced Bob and Ray. They walked out from a door in back of the stage – Bob short and balding, Ray tall with a moustache. My heart flipped. *I'm actually seeing my idols in person.* I thought of Mom again and recalled how disappointed she was at the appearance of her favorite radio personality.

As the pair took their places at a short table with two desk mikes, the audience applauded politely. I wanted to stand and cheer, but restrained myself. Glenn Riggs stood up straight at his microphone, the band began a spirited rendition of "Mention My Name in Sheboygan" and the show was on the air. *Why do I have butterflies?*

As Bob and Ray performed, me, my four buddies plus three people seated in front of us were the only ones who laughed. In one skit, Bob, as a reporter, talked with Ray, the owner of a company that printed calendars.

Bob: So, you're celebrating a big contract?

Ray: Yes. We just shipped ten thousand of our calendars to a chain store in Chicago.

Bob: But looking at your calendar here, I see you've spelled June as "Jure" and you've left the month of August out entirely.

Ray: (Yelling off mike) Call our wives and tell 'em to pack!

The two also did an imaginary remote broadcast in which the reporter's microphone got turned on late by an inattentive engineer.

> Ray: Let's go out to Times Square now where Bob and Ray's man in the field Wally Ballew is standing by to cover the annual Sturdley Day Parade.
>
> Bob: (Silence, then) ... eaking to you from Broadway and 45th Street.

Some people in the audience chuckled when character Mary McGoon, portrayed by Ray in falsetto, began a recipe for a gypsy omelet: "First, steal two eggs."

Another skit required a gunshot. When the sound man's pistol misfired, he got a bigger laugh than Bob and Ray did during the entire show. When the program ended, smiley Glenn Riggs stepped forward again.

"Okay, for the second program now," he said, "we have to pretend it's tomorrow!"

With that, a man in the audience stood up.

"It might as well be the middle of next week for all I care," he said.

He just didn't get Bob and Ray.

* * *

After the broadcast, my buddies and I passed a newsstand on a corner of Radio City. The black and red masthead of a magazine jumped out at me. It was *Broadcasting-Telecasting*, a weekly publication devoted to the business. I bought a copy, buried my nose in it and didn't say a word for the rest of the day.

HALSEY AND THE SILVER MACHINE

In 1952, my father uprooted me from our neat little home on Albert Place. We moved closer to where Marge, our housekeeper, lived with her sister and brother-in-law in Midland Park. Dad bought an old house in Upper Ridgewood, past the fire station on Glen Avenue and away from the mansions with the big lawns. The move made it easier for Marge to get to Dad and me as her hours and days with us were increasing.

The tan stucco house on Van Dyke Street sat behind a wall of cracked field stones and under a row of straggly trees along the side. Dry leaves had blown into the corners of the front porch and dead branches littered the sparse grass of the lawn. In the back, at the end of the gravel driveway, a musty-smelling garage with oil stains on the floor leaned to the left. Inside the house, the baseboards and doors were dark brown, the walls were finished in swirls of rough yellow plaster, and stained light globes clung to the ceilings. Spider webs decorated the corners of the dank basement where Dad set up his workshop.

My bedroom on the second floor had a dormer window facing New York. With money saved from stocking merchandise at Marcus Jewelers after school, I had bought a cheap television receiver from the "Mad Man Muntz" appliance store. Placing the clunky black metal set on a nightstand, I adjusted the rabbit ears antennae only once to bring in decent pictures from all seven stations transmitting off the Empire State Building. Even though Dad had been an avid radio listener in the forties, he hadn't given in to buying a new-fangled television. Still, on Sundays he'd come into my room in his bathrobe to sit on the bed and watch Ed Sullivan.

To get to school in the morning, I walked down past the fire station and caught a ride with fellow student Jack Bennett in a Jeep he painted with our high school colors of maroon and white. To get home in the afternoon, I took a blunt-nosed red and blue diesel bus up from the train station. I missed the sound and smell of the old orange and brown bus with the long snoot that I rode when a kid when living on the east side. The move to Van Dyke Street had one advantage – it put me closer to my buddies who lived on the west side of town, especially one of them.

Halsey Foote Sheffield III had a serious demeanor about him that reminded me of my older brother. His ancestors had founded Sheffield Farms Dairy a century earlier, and the company had grown into a major milk distributor in the Northeast. My new west side friends told me Halsey would inherit a portion of the company's fortune when he turned 21, but I never asked him if that were true.

Halsey lived in his grandmother's three-story Victorian mansion up on a hill in upscale Upper Ridgewood. His father, at leisure all day, tinkered with foreign cars in a barn in back.

"Look at this," Mr. Sheffield said the day I met him. "I just found this beat-up ol' Porsche over in Connecticut."

Halsey's mother, divorced from his dad, lived in a rambling house with a swimming pool in Westwood, New Jersey. My friends and I drove over to visit her as often as we could in the summer, making sure we brought our swim trunks along.

Before I took the test for my driver's license, Halsey let me practice with one of his family's cars. We drove out to a quiet country road in Wyckoff and swapped places on the front seat. While the car wasn't one of the small foreign jobs from the barn, I was happy to get behind the steering wheel of the Sheffield's four-door Pontiac station wagon. Later that week, I demonstrated my driving skill to an officer of the DMV on the straight streets in Hackensack and found it was easier than tooling through the woods of Bergen County. I passed the test with no trouble.

When a semi-formal dance was scheduled at the high school, I admitted to Halsey that I didn't know how to tie a tie. He took two out of his walk-in closet, handed me one and had me face the mirror in his bathroom. Standing next to me, he used the other tie to show the crossover, flip and tuck to make a knot.

"Hold this end and pull the knot up to your neck," he said.

I fumbled until I got a half-assed knot up to my Adam's apple. The tie lay flat on my t-shirt with the skinny end hanging below the wide one by two inches.

"You look dopey," Halsey said.

In his bedroom on the top floor of the mansion was a mint-condition baseball glove, football, telescope and movie camera, but I went right to a silver machine sitting on a book shelf. Caressing the shiny sides of a fat reel-to-reel Wolensak tape recorder, I told him, "Halsey, I gotta try this!"

Stretched out on the floor, I held a little square microphone at my mouth. Halsey pressed the "Play" and "Record" buttons then sat on his bed to listen. When I heard the reels begin to grind, I took a breath and proceeded to record on magnetic tape for the first time.

I started with characters and bits stolen from Bob and Ray. Sounding like I had to blow my nose, I copied Bob

Elliott when he became stopped-up reporter Wally Ballew. Playing all the roles in a spoof of the soap opera *Stella Dallas*, my voice went falsetto for the main character I named *Fort Worth Dallas* just as Ray Goulding's did to portray Mary McGoon.

I even tried selling Lipton Tea like Arthur Godfrey: "By golly, this is good stuff."

My attempts to imitate the New Englander, Irishman, Senator and Jewish lady from *Allen's Alley*, went pretty well – I was pleased I could do them better with my teenage voice than with the squeaky one I had as a kid.

It was hard to wait while Halsey rewound the tape. Sitting up, I hugged my knees and anticipated what was to come. The reels turned again, and my voice came back to me from the speaker holes. I was surprised to hear it had lost the hitch-pitched tightness when I first announced sports news on *Journalism Radio*. I gauged the merit of the nonsense I performed by Halsey's reaction as I recorded it. As we listened to the tape, I could hear his laughter in the background. Right then, I knew I had to use the magnificent recorder again and again. Over the following weeks, I begged Halsey often to let me come to his grandmother's house and record. He gave in every time. Although I thanked him whenever I fooled around with the Wolensak, I don't know if my friend realized how much the silver machine meant to me. I was years away from my goal to be on the radio, but thanks to Halsey Sheffield, my passion was growing stronger.

CLASS ACT

I had two personalities in high school. One was the very outgoing, sit-up-front-and-raise-my-hand-to-answer-every-question type. The other was the silent oh-please-oh-please-don't-call-on-me type.

I enjoyed English and history class, so I was chatty and excelled in both. Chemistry and French made me slink into the back of the rooms and hide behind the students in front of me. Test scores found me out, and I got Ds in chemistry and flunked French. Between tenth and eleventh grade in 1952, I spent July in summer school trying to master the language of my ancestors in France.

* * *

Because I'd heard reports of the war on the living room radio as a kid and had listened when newscasts interrupted music on my bedroom set as a teenager, I was curious about the world. Tenth-grade history disappointed me when it ended with Lincoln's assassination. I wanted to know what caused the Great Depression my parents suffered through and why my father was so against Roosevelt's New Deal. At last, in the eleventh grade, one teacher veered off the rigid history curriculum and the subject became spellbinding.

Bill Slocum was the newest member on the faculty. Younger than other teachers, he was short with broad shoulders, blond hair and a perpetual smile above a sharp chin. On the first day of the school year, he told his class he had served in Army Intelligence during the war. I looked at the kid across the aisle and formed a silent "wow" with my lips.

Slocum told us what led to World War II and why our country was being threatened by Communism. He had us bring in newspaper clippings on Fridays to discuss current events. Once, he stood by his desk, and in a soft voice regaled us with a story of intrigue he experienced in the war.

"I was soaking wet the night I found the farm house in Normandy. I parachuted in there to meet the French resistance and lay out plans for D-Day." We listened and didn't say a word. When he had to get back on track and teach us about the boring Louisiana Purchase, I spoke up: "If you continue with this, we'll have to call you 'Ho Hum Slocum'."

He laughed along with the kids in class.

* * *

My imagination ran wild in English Composition.

Using a school-issued green pencil minus an eraser, I dashed out short stories and poems, then scratched out words and polished phrases with arrows and carets. Thinking I had composed something pretty good, I copied the scribbling neatly to a clean white sheet of lined paper with a ballpoint pen before turning in my work. Mrs. Chynoweth, the teacher, looked at her students over the glasses on her nose.

"Today, I want you to write a dramatic story. Make it mysterious or scary. Use as much description as you can and build the tension."

I got under way with mine, writing it in the form of a radio script. When I handed in my creation, the teacher was either impressed with it or wondered what the hell I had done. The next day, she had me read my story out loud to the class including the directions for music and sound effects.

(Organ: Ominous)

Narrator: (Intense) Beneath the old house, the farmer and his wife gathered their two children in their arms on the floor of the root cellar.
(Sound: Whir, whir, whir)
A weird light grew brighter through the cracks in the door above their heads.
(Organ: Builds and sustains under)
A metallic sound like a thousand insects grew louder and louder.
(Sound: Crackle, crackle, crackle)
A window broke!
(Sound: Crash, tinkle, tinkle)
Great heavy footsteps clumped across the floor.
(Sound: Clump, clump, clump)
The farmer reached for his pitch fork as the door was ripped off its hinges.
(Sound: Crrrunch)
(Organ: Sting)
(Horrified) Hovering over the family, glaring down at them with four red blazing eyes was a monstrous creature. Oily liquid dripped from two mouths.
A white vapor spewed out of nostrils in its forehead.
(Sound: Heavy breathing. Hmmm, hmmm)
The farmer could stand it no longer.

Farmer: Take this, you demon!

Narrator: (Excited) He jabbed his pitch fork up at the form once!

(Organ: Stab)
Twice!
(Organ: Stab, stab)
Three times!
(Organ: Stab, stab, stab)
But to no avail. The monster reared back its ugly head and shot a bolt of lightening into the huddled family below!
(Sound: Whooosh)

Voices: (Screams)

Narrator: (Somber) The family disappeared. The invasion had begun.

(Organ: Up to end)

I got an A+.

NIGHT CALLS

When I could have been dating girls in high school, I visited radio stations.

Sitting next to a quiet classmate in the cafeteria, I discovered he, too, was nuts about radio. Bob Chambers got excited when I suggested we see a station.

"I can use my mom's car this Saturday," he said. "Where should we go?"

I told him I knew where WPAT was in Paterson, but didn't tell him how I had balked at the door as a kid. I was determined to get inside the station that I'd failed to enter six summers ago.

Saturday night, Bob pulled up to the house on Van Dyke Street in his mother's little Nash Metropolitan convertible. The car looked liked an upside-down bathtub, but I fit in nicely and the radio worked.

It was dark when we approached the office building across from the court house on Hamilton Street. The WPAT half was just as I remembered it. Under the glow of a streetlight, the striking red and gold letters on the tall windows were as daunting as before, but I was almost an adult and not a kid anymore. *Surely no one will turn away a person of my age and stature.* Bob was the one who pushed the door bell.

There was no reaction inside. We looked at each other.

"Somebody has to be in there," I said. "What about the announcer we heard on the way down here?"

Turning back to the car, I heard the door click open. When a man stuck his head out, I stammered something to him about wanting to be in radio.

"Can we come in and look around?" I croaked.

He stepped aside, and with a sweep of his hand, motioned for us to enter.

"Where're you both from?" the man asked as we walked down a dark hall of closed doors. I recognized his voice. He was the announcer we'd heard in the car.

"Ridgewood, up in Bergen County," I said.

The carpet ahead was bathed in a soft light from an open door. Bob and I reached it and hesitated.

"Go ahead in, boys," the announcer said.

I took a step up on the raised floor of the station's control room and was met with the sight, sound and smell of radio.

Fluorescent lights in the ceiling lit perforated pale yellow tiles on the walls. Soaring violins played the theme from a movie, and a red pointer stuttered around the face of a clock with each beat of a second. The gray metal casing of a control board on a u-shaped desk gave off a sweet aroma.

An engineer, a heavy gent in a plaid flannel shirt, sat in a chair on wheels, his big stomach pressed against the desk. I moved around in back of him to see the control board.

Black knobs the size of donuts stretched along the bottom and toggle switches stood above each knob, some straight out, some leaning to the right. Black buttons as small as dimes were in a line at the top, a few pushed in, a few left out. In the middle, a thin needle in a glass box danced to the music of the violins. The control board looked intimidating, but I wanted so much to touch it.

From the engineer's position, I looked through slanted windows into three studios. In the smallest one in front of me, a second announcer had his head bent down next to a microphone on a desk stand.

"He's marking up news stories from the teletype down the hall," said the man who had met us at the door. *Could it be the same machine I heard at the open window in the alley when I was a kid?*

To the engineer's left was a studio the size of my bedroom. Our host announcer went in and sat facing the window. A microphone on a boom was inverted, so the letters W P A T across the top hung upside down.

To the engineer's right was a large dark studio, big enough to hold the living room furniture in our house. With light from the control room, I made out a boom mike leaning in to the open top of a grand piano. *Funny, I've never heard the piano played on the station.*

My eyes went back to the engineer who sat between four turntables, two on each side. They were larger than the one on the bulky record changer I inserted in the easel, and the pick-up arms were longer and straighter. As one turntable spun the movie theme, the engineer kept busy with the others. He was setting up music for WPAT's premier evening program, *Gaslight Review.*

I saw him slip a platter from an album cover and, in a flash, fit it perfectly on the little metal spindle of a turntable, placing the needle of the pick-up arm in exactly the right spot. His fingers flew to the control board and snapped a knob, then rotated the platter until a note of music came from under the desk. Turning the platter back an inch, he left it and went to the next turntable and did the same procedure. I watched, fascinated. In spite of the announcers in the two studios and Bob Chambers by my side, I felt like the engineer and I were the only two people in the station.

The announcer in the medium studio looked up and waved his hand.

Through Slanted Windows

"Move away from the window, boys," the engineer said.

When the movie theme ended, he flipped a switch on the control board, and a red glow came on in the hall. He nodded to the announcer, who identified the program and gave the station's call letters and location, his voice resonant, his diction clean. *Man, will I ever sound like that?*

The engineer turned off the switch, flipped on another and nodded to the man in the small studio. Holding pieces of ripped teletype paper, he delivered a newscast with the aplomb of an announcer on a national network. Finishing with the weather for "Northern New Jersey and the New York Metropolitan Area," he launched into a commercial for Lake Hopatcong Heights. I whispered to Bob, "I bet I've heard that one a hundred times."

At the end, he raised a finger and pointed it, the red glow went off in the hall and the engineer pushed a button on a turntable. A love song blossomed from a speaker on the wall. *How smooth. How professional.*

Our host announcer came out of his studio and joined us.

"There's another engineer at our transmitter down the road in Clifton," he said.

Golly, four people to run the station at one time. I compared WPAT in my mind to New York stations. It was smaller, but that's how radio was done in Paterson, New Jersey in 1953.

Not wanting to be pests, Bob and I started to leave. Young – and somewhat nervous of where we were – we didn't think to give our names and shake hands. I did have the manners enough to thank the man who let us in. As I stepped down from the control room, I turned to satisfy my curiosity about one last thing: *What caused the red glow in the hall when the microphones came on?* Above the door was a metal box with two words cut out of the face that were backed by red plastic and a light bulb. I knew then those words were going to mean everything in my life. They said: "On Air."

* * *

I bought a subscription to *Broadcasting-Telecasting*, the magazine I found on the visit to Radio City with my buddies. It was mailed to Dad's house each week filled with more articles and photos than the *Radio Guide* in the Sunday paper.

An article in *B-T* noted that a man named Dickens Wright had been hired from a station in New Haven, Connecticut, to be the general manager at WPAT. As it turned out, he bought a house in Ridgewood, and his daughter was placed in my history class at high school. After talking to her, I discovered who her father was, but I never told her I had visited his station in Paterson or asked if I could come to her home and meet him. If I'd been brave enough, I might have been able to pick the brain of a radio professional and get to know Judy better at the same time. Because I was afraid of rejection, I lost a wonderful opportunity.

* * *

After our experience at WPAT, I was determined to visit more radio stations. It didn't take much to convince Bob Chambers to drive his mother's Nash the following Saturday. The trip to Paterson had been easy, but on the next one, we ventured into a larger, stranger city with no idea where we were going.

As we approached the outskirts, the moon and stars were hidden behind clouds over the forbidding skyline of Newark, New Jersey. I told Bob to pull in to the first gas station we came to, where I checked a phone directory for the two stations I wanted. Jotting the addresses on a crumpled piece of school note paper, I handed it to Bob, who had the good sense to get out and ask directions from the attendant standing at the pumps.

The first station I wanted to visit came in to my bedroom radio at 620 on the dial. It played a hodgepodge of music, and no particular programs or DJs stuck out, but I knew it had studios, microphones and turntables somewhere in Newark – and I had to see them.

Bob navigated the little car by the directions until we were crawling slowly along Newark's busy Central Avenue. For block after block, I looked at numbers on buildings, anxious to get to the one we wanted. Finally, I spotted four chrome letters above the plate-glass window of a piano store – W V N J.

"There it is, Bob!"

I was the one who rang the bell this time. The door was opened by a young man not much older than we were. After I mumbled our reason for being there, he stepped aside and let us in. The three of us walked along a hall without saying a word. Feeling nervous or timid or both, Bob and I didn't ask the young man what he did at the station.

Passing a showroom of potted plants arranged around shiny black pianos, we entered a darkened studio. The only light came through the slanted window of the control room. An engineer sitting inside looked bored as Latin music blared from a speaker. In the corner of the studio was a desk with turntables on either end, one of them spinning a record. A boom mike hung above the desk, and a chair was pulled out, empty.

"Where's the announcer?" I whispered to Bob.

A slim, red-haired man appeared from the hall. With albums tucked under his arm, he clumped across the floor on a crutch. He had only one leg!

"Are you fans of mine?" he asked in a booming voice. I surprised myself by replying with an actual complete sentence.

"No," I blurted, not realizing how curt my answer sounded. "We're interested in radio and we're visiting stations in Jersey."

He frowned at the "no" in my answer, leaned his crutch against the wall and flopped in the chair, the albums splaying out on the table.

Bob and I sat on folding chairs and watched the man cue up a platter from an album on the empty turntable. When music ended on the other one, he signaled to the engineer. A red bulb came on under the control room window.

"Welcome to WVNJ's *Mambo Rendezvous!*" he said. I was too enthralled with the surroundings to catch the humor of a program of dance music hosted by a one-legged man.

In a rumbling bass voice, the announcer read a commercial for the piano store in the front of the building. Bob and I watched him wide-eyed from the edge of our seats. The engineer in the control room, however, stood up, stretched and yawned.

I looked around the studio – seamless linoleum on the floor, small perforated wall tiles and a microphone in the corner with a cord coiled on a hook on its stand. *I wonder what my first studio will look like.*

We listened to the announcer introduce Latin numbers by calling the leaders of the orchestras "Mambo Kings" – Tito Puente, Perez Prado, Desi Arnaz. How different the names were than those I was familiar with – Glenn Miller, Benny Goodman, Tommy Dorsey and all the rest. As maracas shook and trumpets rose and fell, Bob and I headed to the door. I thought enough to say something to the announcer before we left. "Thanks" was the only thing that came out of my mouth.

"Anytime, boys," he said as he went back to shuffling albums.

Out on the street, I looked at the chrome letters above the door.

"Now that's the way the outside of a radio station should look."

Back in the car, Chambers referred to his notes from the gas station attendant and pulled out into traffic.

The second station on the list came in weak at home, scrunched in at 1430 between two foreign languages on the dial. Like WVNJ, it played a mix of music. When my brother was in high school, he listened to Carl Ide spin jazz on the DJ's imaginary boat, *The S.S. Cool*. When I tuned in late at night, I heard a rhythm and blues DJ shout his name backwards through the static: "I am the Bruce called Ramon."

We found the station in a neighborhood of warehouses shut tight for the night. If the street had lights, they were burnt out or busted. The deserted sidewalks were dotted with empty cans, and trash blew along the gutters.

Bob parked the Nash and turned off the headlights. Afraid of what might be lurking in the shadows, we looked cautiously up and down the block. Getting out, we closed the doors carefully, trying not to make a sound.

We hustled across the street to a windowless building with four flat metal letters screwed in to the granite face. Ducking into an alcove, I felt for a small button and pressed it. A chime rang inside WNJR.

One half of double steel doors creaked open, and a man with sad eyes looked out.

Hoping my voice wouldn't quaver, I spoke our request. "Can we come in and look around?"

He held up a crooked finger and wiggled it for us to follow him to a large, two-story studio. Way up on the ceiling, only half the lights were lit, barely illuminating the dull linoleum at our feet. A grand piano sat at one end of the room, its top down, the cover on the keys closed. Against one wall, folded metal chairs leaned haphazardly. On another wall, thick brown drapes were pulled back, exposing bare plaster. The studio had the perfunctory microphone on a stand and a desk mike on a plain wooden table, but it lacked the pizzazz of WPAT. I had told Bob in the car that WNJR was owned by the *Newark Evening News*, so I leaned over to him and whispered, "Maybe this is how a newspaper thinks a radio station should look."

The man acted uninterested with our presence and excused himself. He shuffled off without inviting Bob and me to join him and disappeared through a dark doorway. We looked at each other.

"He must be the announcer we heard in the car," I said, "but where did he go?"

Music sounding like a funeral dirge ended, and a man's voice was heard from high in the ceiling: "You're listening to WNJR's *Music for Musing*." With its recordings of drippy violins and groaning organs, the program was a poor imitation of WPAT's *Gaslight Review*.

"This is weird," I said.

Bob nudged me and motioned with his head to look up. At a slanted window on the floor above, the silhouette of a man stood motionless like a figure in a wax museum.

"Let's get outta here," he said.

Driving back to Ridgewood, the two of us chattered on about who we met and what we saw. We kidded each other by stating our hopes for jobs in radio.

"I want to play mambos and hop around on one leg," Bob said.

"I want to mope around to maudlin music in a mausoleum," I countered.

We laughed as the little car bounced along Route 17.

* * *

Those night visits to stations in Paterson and Newark meant more to me than the NBC tour I took as a kid. I was able to see announcers up close and have them talk to me. I watched records spin, touched sound-proof walls and smelled the aroma of warm equipment. The On Air light at WPAT glowed in my mind and my passion to be on the radio grew even stronger.

THE HAM IS DONE

"You don't seem nervous talking in front of people in class," the cute blonde said to me in the hall at school. She was president of the Nightingales, a group of girls who did volunteer work in pink striped uniforms at the hospital. They were called "candy stripers."

"I have to make an announcement at assembly," she said. "It'll kill me to be up on the stage. Could you do it for me?" I jumped at the chance.

Principal Brown introduced me at Friday's assembly. I walked on stage in front of the curtain, not weak-kneed like I was behind the folds the year before for *Journalism Radio*. Palming a note in my hand with the information, I began with my own rendition, giving in to the temptation for embellishing the announcement.

"I've been told the Nightingales will be selling school beanies and pennants next week by the front doors. They're raising money to buy new 'candy striper' uniforms, so take a hammer to your piggy banks and be ready to buy. We don't want the girls working at Valley Hospital in their gym suits."

The audience laughed, not expecting a little spice to be thrown in. The reaction sent the tingling through me.

Smiling, I walked off the stage to their applause, feeling very much the seasoned professional announcer.

The next week, I was asked by another club to make an announcement. I asked Jerry Wells to join me to add his wacky sense of humor. We were both milk monitors in the cafeteria at the end of lunch period, and as we cleared empty bottles off the tables, Jerry asked me to do something.

"Arch, you gotta meet Norton."

A new student had transferred to Ridgewood High from Ohio. Good-looking with short curly hair and a sly smile, Jim Norton had a quirky air about him. He and I hit it off right away with common interests in Bob and Ray on the radio and Dean Martin and Jerry Lewis movies. Soon, Jim, Jerry and I formed a trio and developed a short, punchy act that kept the student body entertained while getting a message across.

Whenever a request was received to do an announcement for a club, the three of us huddled at lunch time to put together a routine. We'd laughed at the lines we came up with, and other students looked over at us like we were nuts. Before afternoon classes began, we'd sneak into the empty auditorium and rehearse.

At Friday assemblies when Principal Brown said there would be an announcement, the audience burst into applause as Archard, Norton and Wells came out of the wings.

> Jim: The Cooking Club will hold a bake sale by the main doors next Tuesday after school.
>
> Jerry: Oh, boy, devil's food cake, you little devils.
>
> Dave: Certainly not angel food cake from members of *that* group.
>
> Jim: Now cut that out!

It was "High School Harry Humor" for sure, but it got laughs.

* * *

Dave Archard

A tradition at RHS was for the school comedians to be elected to head the Booster Club, so it was no surprise in my senior year that Jim Norton was voted president and I was chosen vice president. Terry Vanderbeck and Barbara Clarke, two level-headed girls, were picked as secretary and treasurer to lend sanity to the organization, and we were able to work Jerry Wells into our high jinx.

During football season, we gathered the student body on the athletic field Fridays after school to rev it up for games the following day. At a Ridgewood High School pep rally in 1953, the cheerleaders jumped around and yelled. Four of the girls got on their hands and knees, three climbed on their backs, and the lightest one scrambled on top to form a shaky pyramid. The band played our fight song, and we sang the words, much to the chagrin of Principal Brown.

"Cheer, cheer for old Ridgewood High.
You bring the whisky, I'll bring the rye."

The football players were introduced, and they stood up from the front row of the bleachers and bowed and waved to great cheers and whistles. Then either Jim, Jerry or I portrayed a representative from the opposing school our team was to play. When it was my turn to be the supposed rep, our team was to go up against Bogota High School.

Located on the banks of the crooked Hackensack River, Bogota, New Jersey, was stuck in the concrete sprawl between the George Washington Bridge and the green trees of Ridgewood. Row houses in the town were homes for many Polish and Italian families, so the high school football team was made up of some pretty rough boys. When Norton introduced me as "Bobby Bogota," I came out to harangue our school, but instead of lumbering like a tough guy, I walked the way Jerry Lewis did on television. With my knees together – and shins below sticking out at an awkward angle – I shouted a greeting like he would.

"Hell-low, everybod-dee."

At the microphone, I imitated the comic actor in his childish voice and trashed everyone associated with RHS. When I called Ridgewood High "a prep school for sissies," the football team rose and started towards me. With arms and legs flailing like Lewis, I took off running and yelling: "Oh, you wouldn't hoit a nice per-sin."

I weaved through the band standing at attention on the field. The crowd laughed and hooted until Bill Dailey, the quarterback, shot at me with the track coach's pistol loaded with a blank. I spun around, clutched my chest and fell face down in the mud on the fifty-yard line. Jack Bennett drove out in his Jeep, loaded my limp body in the back seat and drove off. The crowd cheered loud and long.

The ham was finished cooking.

* * *

I received my biggest laugh in school with a line I didn't mean to be funny. Jim, Terry, Barbara and I asked the principal to let the Booster Club hold a pep rally at night. At first, Dr. Brown was fearful, thinking things would get out of hand, and students would burn down the Village of Ridgewood. After mulling over our request, he relented.

"Okay, you can have a night rally, but there's to be no kidding around when you make the announcement at assembly. I want this to be serious," he said. We agreed.

Friday, Jim addressed the student body from the stage.

"The Booster Club has been approved to hold a special pep rally before the game with Ramsey next week. It's going to be held on the football field Friday night!"

The audience cheered.

Jim went on to explain the necessity for great decorum for safety's sake. He outlined the do's and don't's laid down by Dr. Brown. That's when I spoke up.

"Hermance Place in front of school will be closed to car traffic the night of the rally. There'll be a chain across the street to remind you."

The audience roared. With a quizzical look on my face, I looked over at the wings, up to the balcony, then to Jim. I shrugged as the laughter continued.

* * *

At the end of football season, the Booster Club put on a Saturday night celebration dance in the cafeteria. Jim, the girls and I made it a special affair by hiring a professional band from North Jersey. Between numbers, Norton and I got on the bandstand to welcome the students and their dates and to introduce the team. When we finished, I turned to Jim.

"Could I say one more thing?" I asked.

"Sure," Norton said.

I turned to the saxophone player in the band.

"Are you really Zoot Sims?" He was a popular bebop musician of the day.

The crowd on the dance floor didn't get it, but the band laughed.

HIGH TIMES

John McCutcheon, the portly teacher with a quick wit and ready smile, became deadly serious when he hammered the basics of news writing into his journalism students.

"Get the 'who,' 'what,' 'where,' and 'when' in the first paragraph and don't start your story with the word 'the'."

Having taken the required two years of English as a sophomore and junior, I was able to choose another course when a senior. I chose journalism. It was a good decision because McCutcheon taught me how to write concisely, the way I would have to in a radio commercial with strict time constraints. Because the school newspaper, *High Times*, was published every week, I also learned the discipline of working under the pressure of deadlines. The word "high" meant something different in 1953, so no one snickered at the name of our paper.

Every Monday, I was given an assignment by the student editor-of-the-week. I had to track down a teacher or staff member for my story and have a serious conversation. If I had to interview a student, it was usually over a sandwich during lunch. I got to know interesting kids I never would have talked to otherwise.

Tuesday, I wrote my story, struggling with the rules by Mr. McCutcheon. *How can I begin without using "the?" I must get the four Ws in the lead.* It took repeated trips to the pencil sharpener and the rubbing with a gum eraser to get it right.

Wednesday, I handed my story to the student editor who passed it on to Mr. McCutcheon. The teacher slashed it with a red pen and sent me back to my desk to try again. When he read my rewrite, he looked up.

"Good, laddie."

A classmate banged out my story on a typewriter. I took typing class, but never got the knack of using all my fingers, so I was slow. I sat and watched as my words came alive in straight black lines on crisp white paper.

Thursday morning, campus news, sports, gossip, editorial and photos – plus ads from merchants in town – were gathered together. I beat the editor-of-the-week to the front seat of McCutcheon's car and felt important holding the entire edition on my lap as we rode to a printer in Pompton Lakes.

Friday morning, we went back to the printer and loaded bundles of the paper in the trunk, the smell of ink filling the car. *High Times* hit the hallways at lunchtime for the bargain price of a dime.

* * *

Dorothy Collins, the perky singer on TV's *Your Lucky Strike Hit Parade* in 1954, was asked by the Ridgewood Women's Club to be emcee for a fashion show at the high school auditorium. Girls in the senior class were models, and they sneaked me backstage the night of the show.

Dorothy Collins walked on and off the stage to introduce each segment. I was standing in back of her in the wings when the petite blonde turned around and spoke to me.

"How am I doing?" she asked.

I was surprised she asked me, a skinny kid in t-shirt and chinos, but I didn't hesitate. In my best grown-up voice, I answered.

"You're doing okay."

* * *

Mr. O'Meara, the mild mannered art teacher, approached me in his class as I stood at my easel smearing oil paint around.

"You're, uhhh, pretty good at drawing. We, ummm, need someone to draw something on television. Do you think, ahhh, that's something you could do?"

My answer shot out.

"Sure!"

Our student council officers were invited to appear on WATV Channel 13 in Newark. Mr. O'Meara recruited me to create a pie chart on camera as the officers talked about different slices of school life. I practiced drawing a circle right away.

By reading *Broadcasting-Telecasting* cover-to-cover each week, I learned that a TV station had to promise the Federal Communications Commission it would air some "educational programming" to keep its license. Most stations buried it on Sunday morning, but WATV scheduled our program on a weeknight opposite quiz shows and sitcoms on the networks. We were going on live in prime time!

The evening of the broadcast, officers, faculty advisor and I arrived at a dinghy theater on Broad Street in Newark. WATV's revenue wasn't as big as stations across the Hudson in New York and had to fill its schedule with old cowboy movies and commercials for mail-order merchandise. The building for the station wasn't as glamorous as Channel 4 in the RCA Building with people scurrying in and out under the gray and silver overhang spelling "NBC

STUDIOS." From the street, the theater housing Channel 13 looked deserted.

We stopped in the dimly lit lobby and a woman appeared from the light of an office door.

"Follow me," is all she said.

Keeping up with her brisk pace through a darkened hall, we reached a thick door and she pushed it open. I was amazed to discover a full-fledged, well-equipped, very modern television studio.

One half was lit by banks of bright Klieg lights overhead. Peering in the dark end, I recognized the set for *Uncle Fred's Fun House* and stifled a laugh. I didn't want my peers to know I watched the kiddy show a few times.

There was no slanted window of a control room and I knew why. From my reading, I'd learned there is no need for visual access to a television studio. A director down a hall or up a floor could see the action on monitors. Channel 13's control room had to be somewhere in the building. I wanted to find it, but I had a show to do.

I approached the area our group was to use. Technicians rolled three cameras back and forth on pedestals and aimed the lenses at a table, chairs, world globe and American flag. A microphone on a long boom arm hung over the arrangement from a platform on four truck tires. I hesitated before going under the lights, and my stomach flip-flopped.

This is big time television!

A man holding a clipboard told the council officers to sit at the table. He ordered me to set-up my easel and pointed to a yellow X taped on the floor.

"Put it there."

A man stepped out of the dark end of the studio and spoke to the officers.

"Sit up straight and answer the questions clearly."

He shot a glance at me.

"Draw your pie slices quickly and boldly," he said before rushing off. I dug in my pocket to make sure I hadn't left my marking pen in the car.

A bald man with glasses appeared, said he was the moderator and sat at the table. Somebody yelled "Quiet," the cameramen snapped to attention, and a red light atop the middle camera flashed on. The man with the clipboard threw a finger cue, and the program went on the air. Neat, clean, professional.

The moderator fired questions, and the officers answered smoothly. When a camera swung to me, I held the pad tight with one hand and drew my circle. It came out a little egg-shaped, but the pad didn't fall off, the easel didn't collapse, and the pen didn't run dry. After I drew a slice on the pie chart, I turned and gawked at a camera. Neat, clean, professional.

As the program progressed, an eerie feeling came over me. There was no sound in the studio except for the chitchat of the moderator and the officers. The cameramen worked in silence, their cameras making no noise. The man with the clipboard said nothing into the small microphone attached to his earphones. I kept thinking how our images were going over to the Empire State Building in Manhattan and flying out to millions of TV sets in the tri-state area.

On the ride back to Ridgewood, we all jabbered on about our show biz experience. I had to wear a tie and jacket for my TV debut, but I knew disc jockeys could wear whatever they wanted when they were on the air. *I'll stick with being in radio.*

* * *

Outrageous articles and staged photos made up the gag issue of *High Times*. It poked fun at school glamour girls, football players, faculty and coaches, so the students looked forward to the annual edition every January. When the journalism class returned from Christmas in 1954, I was chosen editor-in-chief.

Mr. McCutcheon happened to be laid up in the hospital when we put together the four pages of hilarity. Because his guidance and censorship were absent, the inmates took over and ran the asylum.

I renamed the paper *Hip Times* and designed the masthead. With stick pen and India ink, I drew a sleazy man peeking around an old fashioned flash camera above the slogan: "We dig the most in dirt."

My staff sat at their desks with pencils poised as I paced in front of them, all of us hoping an idea would pop into someone's head for the front page. Peter Faber raised his hand.

"Yeah, Pete, whadda ya got?" I said, trying to sound like the editor of a big city daily.

"Since a couple of kids have been caught smoking on campus," he said "why don't we uncover a great cigarette scandal?" The staff nodded and began throwing out ideas.

"We could make up phony accounts of smoke billowing out of the boys' and girls' rooms whenever the doors are opened," said one.

"How about an interview with a student on the pleasure of lighting up after a satisfying dish of tuna casserole in the cafeteria," said a second. We laughed.

"There's a guy who sits next to me in chemistry," said a third. "He says he sneaks a smoke after lunch behind the auto mechanics shop. Why don't we see how many Pall Malls we can stick in his mouth and take his picture?" We laughed louder, and pencils began to write.

Using the mystical radar in the school office, a staff member tipped off the principal to what we were doing. Dr. Brown came in the classroom the following morning and made us pull the smoking idea. Deadline was approaching and we had to come up with something else – and fast.

That night, I saw a story in Dad's *Journal American* about Arthur Godfrey. In addition to his daily radio show, he hosted *Talent Scouts* on both radio and television on Monday nights and reigned over his little Godfrey's Wednesday on television. I listened to his Saturday radio program once and discovered it was only recorded excerpts from the daily show. Godfrey seemed to be on the air all the time.

To avoid being mobbed by his adoring fans on a commercial flight, he became a licensed pilot and flew his own plane. While attempting to fly out of Teterboro Airport in the Jersey swamps, Godfrey was delayed by runway traffic. When finally allowed to take off, he circled his plane, dove toward the control tower in anger and then flew away. His buzzing of the tower was splashed across the front pages of New York papers. The next morning, I related the incident to my staff.

"Why don't we have Al Mayhew become 'Arthur' Mayhew," I said. Al was known by the student body for his stunts at lunch and during fire drills, so he was perfect for the part.

"We'll say 'Arthur' was piloting an experimental plane he built in wood shop when he buzzed the school bell tower. To make him resemble Godfrey, let's make Mayhew the star of the *Horn and Hardart Children's Hour* on Channel 4."

The staff loved it. Ideas began to ricochet and we got to work. While I crafted the lead story, Adrienne Arps created phony eyewitness accounts of "Arthur" banking his wooden plane toward the school. Warren Butler wrote a bogus interview with a janitor who gave the count of dead pigeons he had to clean up after the buzzing.

We took a picture of Mayhew seated at a mock news conference with reporters pressing around him holding note pads and microphones. I told Al to use his hands to show how his plane was blown toward the bell tower by a gust of wind, just as Godfrey did in his picture in the papers. The photo ran on the front page of "Hip Times" under a bold headline.

TV STAR IN TOWER BUZZ
Plane Routs Pigeons

We made up other silly stuff with much glee. The sports guys on staff developed a story of the captain on our basketball team throwing games for bookies so he could buy his girlfriend a mink sweatshirt. One of the girls created a tear-filled column called "Letters to the Lovelorn." Even merchants in town who bought regular ads let us have fun with their copy: "Our shoes squeak, leak and reek. Meyerson Shoe Store downtown."

Hip Times was a smash. The day it came out, Dr. Brown stopped in the classroom to congratulate us. Returning to school the next week, Mr. McCutcheon wiped his brow in relief when he saw what we had done.

* * *

McCutcheon brought us all up short one day when he told us "A politician's first job is to get re-elected."

We were aghast. As future journalists ready to shape opinions and change the world, we thought his statement was harsh. Throughout the course, he made other pronouncements about government and society that were shocking at the time, only to be revealed as true later in my life.

WORKING TOWARD A GOAL

"Y'know, I can't afford to send you to college."

My father's statement shocked me. I had mentioned to him that I was to meet with the guidance counselor at high school to discuss my plans after graduation. Every year, the Bergen County School Board boasted that ninety-eight percent of graduating seniors at RHS went on to higher education and I was expected to be among them in 1954.

Anger filled me. When my brother graduated from high school four years ahead of me, Dad could afford to fly with him to Syracuse University and stay in a hotel for Tom's audition at the music school there. He paid for Tom's books, dorm room and meals for a whole semester. *I don't understand why there's no money now that it's my turn to go.*

When Packard joined with Hudson, Dad was brought along and given a company car. The Hudson Pacemaker glided over the bumps of Route 17 when my father drove into work in Manhattan, and the low, wide, four-door sedan was a great prom date car for me. Later on, however, the two car companies merged with Nash to form American Motors. Dad was 52 at the time and he was shut out. It was probably because of his age as it had been with GM after the war, but I didn't hear my father give a reason. Before he had to leave the company, he was allowed to buy a smaller Hudson Jet at a discount. *Big deal.*

Dad had to find another way to make living, so he answered an ad in a do-it-yourself magazine and bought the necessary equipment to start his own business. He was finally going to work with his hands, but not in wood.

Lining up a row of rubber molds on his work bench in the basement, he scooped powder into a bowl from bags of plaster and something called alum. Adding water, he whipped the mixture into a white glop and poured it in holes at the top of each mold. After the mixture hardened, he pulled the molds apart and out popped eight-inch tall snow-white oriental figurines. Marge and I made them come alive – using tiny brushes, we painted faces, hair and costumes on their shiny bodies.

My father visited gift shops in North Jersey and received orders for the figurines, but the business barely made enough money to support the household. When I heard him grouse to Marge when bills had to be paid, it dawned on me. *He's broke or is broken by the automobile business.*

* * *

Sitting in the office of the school guidance counselor, I gazed out the window then turned to her.

"I want to be in radio," I said.

She reached around and pulled brochures off a credenza.

"There are many fine colleges and universities throughout the country with excellent communication departments," she said thumbing through the slick material. My grades were sprinkled with only one and two A's and I didn't play on the football team, so scholarships were out of the question. Dad couldn't pay for college, but I resisted the urge to tell the woman she was wasting her time. Accepting the brochures, I thanked her and left the office.

As I walked down the hall, I realized I didn't want to spend the next four years of my life in college anyway. *I want to get into radio as soon as possible.* Pausing at the stairs, I ditched the brochures in a trash can.

* * *

The words "disc jockey" jumped out at me from an ad in the back pages of *Broadcasting-Telecasting.* A sixteen-week course at a school in New York was all it took to become a spinner of records. After learning microphone technique and the operation of studio equipment, graduates were guaranteed placement at radio stations. I realized a diploma from a college wasn't necessary to get into radio in 1954. It just took graduation from the Columbia School of Broadcasting.

That Saturday, I helped my father outside the house, picking up dead limbs fallen from the scraggly trees and raking dry leaves off what grass there was in the yard. When we needed a break, we sat on the steps by the kitchen door. Taking a deep breath, I began to voice my plan.

"Dad, I want to go to a broadcasting school in New York when I graduate from Ridgewood High. I figure I can get a job and earn the money. Is it okay if I stay here at home?" I bit my lip waiting for his answer.

My father was quiet for a moment then frowned and looked at the musty-smelling garage leaning at the end of the driveway.

"That sounds all right," he said. "Go inside and get me a beer." I rose from the steps. "And get one for yourself." I bounded into the house.

Leaning against the refrigerator, I felt relief that I had overcome the first hurdle of my plan. The next step was critical. *Mobility. I need a car.*

* * *

With meager pay from the after-school job at Marcus Jewelry, I was able to save a small stash of money in my sock drawer. Arriving on a bus at *Check with Chick* used cars in Hawthorne, I found a 1941 Plymouth in the back row of the lot. One word and the price were scrawled in white shoe polish across the windshield: "Bargain $45."

The seats in the black two-door coupe had tears in the upholstery, and the sun visor on the passenger side was missing. To start the engine, I had to push a worn rubber knob above the gas pedal with my right foot. Depressing the clutch pedal with my left, I shifted gears with the long rod with a knob sticking up from the hump on the floor.

Driving the car around the block before buying it, I made sure the radio worked.

* * *

After graduating from Ridgewood High School in June of 1954, I was surprised to learn what my two best buddies were earning at summer jobs before leaving for college. Bill Dailey and Halsey Sheffield bragged they were making seventy-five dollars a week each at the A & P warehouse in East Paterson. Dailey, the son of an A & P executive, was going to Lafayette University, and Sheffield, an heir to a milk fortune, was enrolled at Cornell – and they were each pulling in seventy-five smackers a week. *How unfair!*

I called Bill's father and asked him what job could I get with A & P? Mr. Dailey said he'd call the manager at the store in Ridgewood and told me to stop in Monday. Hanging up the phone, it hit me. *Why didn't I ask for one of the lucrative jobs at the warehouse? What a dope.*

I began working the following week at the A & P food store where my mother shopped during the war. My pay was thirty-five dollars a week.

THE GREAT ATLANTIC AND PACIFIC TEA COMPANY

Four sets of tracks for the Erie Railroad ran in back of a building with the round, red A & P logo. The store was south of the station in Ridgewood, but I didn't see trains or much of anything. Like the job at the jewelry store, I was in the basement.

Cartons of cans, crates of vegetables and cases of soda arrived all too soon from trucks at the delivery door. The stock was sent rattling down to the basement on metal wheels of a long chute, and I had to catch it before it flew off and smashed on the concrete floor. At lunch time, I sat on a pile of wooden pallets in the damp storage room and ate my sandwich under the glare of a lone light bulb.

Before long, I was brought upstairs and handed a white apron and a box cutter by a gray-haired man with thick glasses and a bum leg. The red apron he wore indicated he was the senior stock clerk. The man had worked there from the day the store opened in the 1930s.

"Slice the tops off the cartons in the aisles," he said, handing me a clipboard.

"Read the sheets on this and stamp the prices on the merchandise. Be sure you put the cans and boxes by their proper tags on the shelves." He limped away.

I dragged a cart of wooden handles across the store's warped floor to an aisle stacked with merchandise. The end of each handle showed a price on a rubber tip. After opening cartons, I hit a blue ink pad with the correct price and smacked it on a can lid or box top. As I repeated the process over and over, I repeated a thought over and over –

This job is going to get me to the DJ school. I didn't want to stay at the store until I was a gray-haired man wearing a red apron.

On Friday, my wages were sealed in a small yellow envelope and placed with my punch card next to the time clock. No folded paycheck was inside, just cash and coins. As I dumped out the money, there was a tap on my shoulder. The smiling union shop steward was at my side with his hand out. To keep my job at the grocery store, I had to join the Newark Local of the Meat Cutters Union. With taxes out and dues paid, I took home a few bills and a handful of silver. After buying gas for the Plymouth, I put what was left in a glass Mason jar labeled "DJ School" in my bedroom.

In the corner of the A & P, a round little bookkeeper worked in a booth with glass walls. The booth was three steps off the floor, so she could watch the shoppers in the aisles. One day, the woman came down from her perch and took me by the hand. She marched me to the front of the store.

"You're going to be a checker," she announced.

After the bookkeeper gave me instructions, shoppers bumped their wire carts into my check-out lane and piled groceries on a dented metal shelf. Pulling each item toward me, I read the price and pressed buttons from zero to nine on the front of an upright cash register. The amount jumped up mechanically in a little window at the top. I took the customers' money, punched a square key with the heel of my hand and stepped back. A drawer full of cash and coins flew out, and the total showed in the window. After counting a customer's change out loud, I bagged the groceries. The first time I packed a brown paper sack, the little old lady I was serving looked up at me through squinty eyes.

"Put the loaf of bread *on top* of the cans, thank you very much."

At the end of my first shift, I watched the bookkeeper close out my register. She pressed a button on the side of the register. It whirred and spit a long thin strip of paper from a slot.

"These are all the transactions you did today," she said.

She punched the square key with the heel of her hand, and the cash drawer came flying out. Instead of stepping back as I did, she turned and stopped it with her hip.

Counting the bills and coins in the tray, she scribbled the figures on the strip of register paper and did the math.

"Good, sweetie." she said. I was proud of myself. The new position was like being promoted to management. While someone else was on the floor stamping cans and boxes, I got to handle money.

On the following Monday when my shift ended, the bookkeeper looked up from her figures.

"Oops. Not good. Ten dollars short."

Although she trained me to count change out loud, I must have given a shopper too much money back. The next day, the amount came up short by ten dollars again.

"Bad," the bookkeeper said. *What's going on? I make sure I lock the register before going on a break. Could someone else have a key?*

By Wednesday, Mr. Garofolo, the manager, hovered over the bookkeeper as she figured my day's activity. I looked at the ceiling. *Oh, please let it come out right.* They straightened up, and the manager put his hand on his forehead and dragged it down over his face.

"A twenty dollar shortfall," the bookkeeper said, her voice solemn.

On Friday, Mr. Garofolo stopped to me in the stock room before I went home.

"Dave, you're being transferred to our store in Suffern. The manager up there has more patience than I do."

His words hit me like a punch. Being young, I didn't speak up and say someone might have been dipping into my cash drawer. I accepted that the shortages were my fault. With head down, I pulled off my apron and dropped it in the laundry hamper.

"I'm getting too old for this," the manager muttered as I left the store.

* * *

The A & P across the state line in Suffern, New York was a short drive up Route 17 from Ridgewood. The staff at the store welcomed me like a long-lost child. *Are they sorry I got a raw deal in Ridgewood, or have they been short a checker and here I am?* I tied on an apron and walked to an assigned cash register with a feeling of confidence. In the first week at the new store, the cash drawer came out on the nose at the end of my shift. Driving home everyday, I rolled down the window in my Plymouth and sang to tunes on WNEW.

One afternoon after work, I was tempted to visit a radio station. Even though *White's Radio Log* showed WGNY in nearby Newburgh, New York, I decided not to go – I would concentrate on my job at the A & P and save money for the DJ school.

One day as I was listening to Martin Block on my commute, I heard him play a new record that sounded different than the other pop tunes. Reaching over, I turned up the volume on the dashboard radio. By blending layers of guitars, all his, with voices, all hers, Les Paul and Mary Ford played and sang "How High the Moon." I read how the husband and wife recorded the song on multiple tracks of tape at their home in Mahwah, New Jersey. The town was minutes away from Suffern, but I didn't venture to find the house and see the studio. *Who'd answer the door if I did? Les or Mary?*

* * *

After hearing my complaints about the wages at the A & P, Marge, our housekeeper, suggested I call a friend of her family.

"He owns a dental lab in Fairlawn and might need someone," she said.

I called and was elated to be hired. With an increase of ten dollars a week and no union dues, I gave my notice to the manager at the A & P. On the last day in Suffern, I jumped and clicked my heels going to my car – and almost fell. *All right! I'm getting closer to the DJ school.*

Delivering false teeth and returning with gum impressions didn't require the brain work than making change at the food store did. In the morning, I drove the Plymouth to a little building on Route 4. Two men in long white coats, the owner and his assistant, worked side by side in a cramped lab. They had paper bags waiting for me with names and addresses of dentists stapled to each one. I snatched keys off a hook, loaded their Ford coupe parked outside and started off.

The first week on the job was a mess. Frustrated with trying to find dentists' offices, I bounced the company car over median strips on the highway, made u-turns on busy streets and turned around on driveways in residential areas. I tried not to panic.

A crumpled map stuffed in the glove compartment didn't help. It covered the entire state of New Jersey and only showed the major roads in Bergen County. I didn't dare ask the men at the lab for directions. They might have wondered why they hired me.

By the next Monday, I had figured out the best ways to the dentists by using short cuts through alleys and side streets. Relaxing, I enjoyed a pleasant routine. Pretty receptionists greeted me by name, and I got to know theirs. The radio stayed on as I drove from office to office. In the morning, I marched around the breakfast table with Don McNeill in my mind and imitated the sliding trombone that played every fifteen minutes on *Arthur Godfrey Time*. In the afternoon, I tapped the steering wheel as I sang along to songs and jingles on WNEW. A box of Milk Duds on the front seat kept me fueled.

At lunch time, I ate a sandwich at the end of the work bench and watched the two men place false teeth in fake gums. The aroma of the pink compound they used to make the bridgework filled the lab and the Ford. My clothes smelled like it at the end of the day.

MIXING RADIO WITH WORK

    Bright sunshine and the trill of a bird woke me Saturday morning. I looked between the curtains of the dormer window. The sky was clear and blue. Monday through Friday belonged to the dental lab, but the weekends were all mine. *What a great day to visit a radio station.*
    Snapping the radio alive on the nightstand, I rolled the needle to frequencies lined up tight toward the end of the dial. A faint signal crackled in, jammed between rhythm and blues and a man speaking Chinese. An announcer identified the mystery station, and I found it in *White's Radio Log.* WNRC had its microphones and turntables somewhere in New Rochelle, New York, and I wanted to see them.
    After breakfast, I said good bye to Dad and Marge, headed out the door and jumped in my car. The way to New Rochelle was across the Hudson River and up from the city. The Plymouth was too old to get me there, so I drove it to the logical starting point, the Erie Railroad station in Ridgewood. By noon, I was on a train headed north from Grand Central Station, "crossroads of a million private lives."
    Beyond the confusion of tenements in the Bronx, the scenery turned to the golf course grass and slender birch trees of Westchester County. The train glided in to New

Rochelle, and I hopped off. Finding a pay phone inside a candy store, I looked up the radio station in the directory. The girl behind the counter pointed me in the right direction, and I started off on foot.

As I walked along a row of clothing and gift boutiques, I saw foreign sports cars pull up and well-dressed women with perfect hairdos get out for their Saturday shopping. When the street changed to homes with manicured lawns and flowers, I stopped at a curbside mailbox with four letters painted on the side: W N R C.

Branches from a large gnarled tree loomed over a shabby cottage tucked behind a bed of short brown evergreens. It brought to mind a line from a poem in school. *How did it go? "Under a spreading chestnut tree, the village smithy stands."* There was no man in overalls out front holding a hammer, but the building for WNRC looked like a shade-tree operation to me. I pressed a bell, and a guy my age in t-shirt and chinos opened the door.

"I'm Dave from over in Jersey. I want to be in radio. Can I come in and look around?" He scratched his crew cut with eyeglasses clutched in his hand and motioned with the other to follow him. We walked a few steps along a narrow hall and entered the station's control room.

A u-shaped table was crammed between shelves overflowing with records, albums, books and magazines. A control board sat on the plywood top of the table, a sweating can of Pepsi next to it. Two turntables were flush with the wings of the table, one of them spinning Johnny Ray's "Walkin' My Baby Back Home." The afternoon sun streamed in from a row of windows. Squinting through a pane, I saw the thick trunk of the tree outside. A breeze blew the branches and shadows of leaves moved on the worn carpet at my feet.

I felt bolder than I had on the visits to stations in Paterson and Newark, so I returned to the hall to nose around. The announcer, reading a magazine, didn't say a word.

Through Slanted Windows

A chunka-chunka-chunka sound drew me to a flimsy accordion door. Folding it back, I discovered a teletype machine. As the letter sticks beat out words on yellow paper in a staccato rhythm, the metal housing rocked on four thick legs. After each line of information ended, the paper was pushed up high enough for me to read it. Placing my hand on the machine, I felt a thrill as I scanned news stories about events around the world.

I looked under the belly of the machine to see the paper feeding in from a long box between its legs. Other boxes were stacked waist high on both sides of the teletype, each one ready to be pulled out, opened up and a continuous sheet of paper inserted from it into the machine when the current supply ran out. *That's something I'll have to do at my first station.*

I picked up a spool of black ribbon wrapped in cellophane from the shelf above. *I guess a new ribbon has to be put in the teletype when words get too light.* A rag with ink stains was bunched-up by other spools. *It must be a messy job.*

A coffee maker sat on the next shelf. Black liquid coated the bottom of the glass carafe, and unwashed cups were jammed next to it, one with a lipstick smear on the rim.

Let's see. Feed paper in teletype, change ink ribbons and make coffee. I worried I might foul up doing those tasks. *I'm learning there's more to radio than playing records and talking on the air.*

At the end of the hall, I stopped at a gray transmitter the size of the soda machine opposite it. Fat tubes glowed behind a thick glass window, and the innards hummed. A clipboard hung from a nail on the paneled wall next to the transmitter, a stack of printed forms held tight by the clamp. A ballpoint pen dangled at the end of a string thumb tacked to the paneling. Looking at the top form on the clipboard, I guessed the numbers scribbled in the columns were meter readings of the transmitter.

Cigarette butts lay scattered around a dented metal waste can overflowing with balled up paper. *Somebody missed the basket when emptying an ashtray. Is that another job I'll have to do?*

On a work bench splattered with drops of paint, the tip of a soldering iron poked its nose out from a heap of wires and switches. The speaker from a radio lay naked on top of a stack of faded engineering magazines. *Man, is this how my first station will look?*

Standing by the back door, I looked past a rusty thermometer mounted on a porch pillar and saw the station's tower in the backyard. Two hundred feet of steel held straight by wires was all WNRC needed to radiate its signal to the good folks of New Rochelle. *I'm lucky I can pick up anything in Ridgewood from here.*

Returning to the control room, I gazed through a long window into a room with knotty pine paneling. The announcer looked up from his magazine.

"That's the manager's office," he said. "We use it when the mayor comes in to do his program on Saturday morning." The glass of the window was not slanted.

I stood behind the announcer and imagined myself seated at the u-shaped table. A microphone, the type used in booths at ballparks, hung from a pipe bending over the control board. A plug-in alarm clock on an extension cord sat on top, a second hand sweeping the small hard-to-read numbers on the face.

A wire ran up the wall to a chipped wooden speaker, and from behind its tattered fabric came the sound of the Four Lads finishing "Moments to Remember." The announcer put down his magazine, took a swig from the Pepsi can and sat up. Careful not to bump his chair, I stepped closer and leaned over.

The record ended, and with a flick of a finger, he turned on the microphone switch. Standing in back of him, I flicked my finger, too. A red light bulb went on above the desk.

"It's 1:20 and 75 degrees on this sunny Saturday at WNRC."

As he spoke, I thought of what I would say if I was at the microphone. My eyes went up as he raised his head to look at a notebook propped on a shelf above the control board. My lips moved silently with every word he read from a public service announcement for U.S. Savings Bonds. My hand moved with his to another turntable.

"Margaret Whiting is joined by Jimmy Wakely now, and they're 'Slippin' Around.'" He started the record, turned off the mike and slouched back in the chair. I was thrilled to have been so close to being on the air.

"Did you go to a broadcasting school?" I asked the announcer.

"Nah, I just work here on weekends. I'm going to NYU and studying political science." I thanked him and left.

Walking to the train, I looked back at the large tree over WNRC. Its limbs seemed to be hugging the little radio station.

* * *

Delivering false teeth for the dental lab was easy. I worked there for two months, but complained about my pay when I got home every Friday. The "DJ School" jar wasn't getting green quick enough.

Marge told me about a cousin of hers who worked as a maintenance man at a chemical factory: "Give Dennis a call. Maybe there's an opening."

I did and he suggested I apply at the factory and mention his name. The following Monday, I was hired with an increase of ten dollars a week.

FACTORY FACTS

Located on the banks of a stagnant river in Paterson, New Jersey, the Ultra Chemical Company was a drab building of corrugated steel walls and narrow broken windows under a rusty tin roof. A brick smokestack burped puffs of gray smoke that drifted off beyond the leafless trees on the road down from Hawthorne.

I stood next to sour-looking men older than my father in a dreary room that smelled like soap. They wore flannel shirts with the sleeves rolled up, thick boots laced up to their knees, and bib overalls with packs of Camels and Luckies jammed in the front pockets. I was dressed in a fresh pair of dungarees, still stiff from the store, a t-shirt and my high school gym sneakers.

While we waited at a black rubber conveyer belt, I listened, but didn't express shock as the men joked and called each other names. There was a "Mick" and a "Pollack" and a little dark man they called an "I-Tie." Two Negro men stood down the line and said nothing.

A bell sounded, and the belt started to move. Brown jars of floor wax with green and white labels came out from a window in a wall. The man at the head of the line took an "I Love Lucy" promotional sticker from a box and wet it on a sponge. He snatched the first jar off the belt, slapped the sticker on the corner of the label and put the jar in a divided cardboard carton. The next man did the same with the second jar. When the third one came down, it was my turn.

I wet a sticker with my sponge, put Lucille Ball's head and endorsement on the jar and placed it in the carton at my feet. When it was full, a man with a hump on his back put the carton on a fork lift facing the shipping department.

After an hour of wetting, sticking and packing, the bell rang again, the belt stopped and a shout came through the window in the wall: "Break!"

When I tried to buy a bottle of Orange Crush from a soda machine, my sticky fingers couldn't get the coins in the slot.

"Go in the shit house and wash your hands," growled the I-Tie man waiting in back of me.

* * *

A week later, I was pulled off the conveyer belt by the shipping boss and sent upstairs. A foreman with pants snapped tightly under his beer belly was waiting. He thrust a broad-blade shovel at me and said to stand on a metal grate. He cupped his mouth and shouted.

"Okay, let 'er rip!" White soap powder billowed out from a chute and drifted around my sneakers.

"Push that stuff over the grate," the foreman said. "And don't spit in it." I did what he said until no more powder came down and what was left on the grate had disappeared at my feet. I found out later the "stuff" went to the level below where it was boxed and shipped as the laundry detergent "All."

When I got home that day, I didn't need a cake of soap in the shower. I just lathered naturally.

* * *

Every day at lunch time, the men tucked napkins in their overalls, snapped open black metal lunch pails and dug for thick sandwiches of pumpernickel bread filled with slabs of ham and bologna dripping with yellow mustard. I pulled out my peanut butter and jelly sandwich on Wonder Bread from a plain brown bag. While they poured steaming dark coffee into the cups of their Thermos bottles, I drank Yoo Hoo chocolate drink from a waxed cardboard container.

I would sit and listen to the men talk between mouthfuls. They complained about wives, kids and house payments, bragged about fish they caught and quarreled over baseball teams. Being young and single, I had nothing to offer. If I chimed in and said I wanted to be a disc jockey on the radio, they would have hooted me off the loading dock. *I wonder if these men had dreams of doing something else before being stuck here in the jobs they have.*

* * *

Workers at the conveyer belt called the shipping boss "Ole, the Swede." I didn't dare call him that. To me he was "Mr. Olson." On cold, wet days, he often handed me a pair of thick gloves and sent me to work outside. In the drizzle of rain under a leaden winter sky, I crushed damaged cardboard boxes and threw them in the roaring fire of an incinerator. The red On Air light at WPAT glowed in the flames before me.

JAZZBO, MOONDOG AND JOHNNY

So I'm on the corner of Fifth Avenue and 45th Street in Manhattan. Bored at home Saturday, I had jumped the train and gone into the city. I stared at the building across the street. Inside was my favorite radio station, WNEW.

A paunchy man with horn-rimmed glasses and neatly-trimmed goatee stopped beside me and waited for a traffic light. I recognized him from the autographed postcard he had mailed me after I'd sent him a fan note. *My favorite disc jockey on WNEW is standing right next to me!* In a flash of courage, I stuck out my hand.

"Hi. I'm Dave Archard from New Jersey. I listen to you all the time. Are you going over to the station for your show?"

"Yeah. Would you like to join me?"

"Oh, yes." My answer embarrassed me for sounding like an old lady.

"Come in the lobby in fifteen minutes and give your name to the receptionist."

The light changed, Al "Jazzbo" Collins stepped off the curb and hustled over to the radio station. I remained on the sidewalk, flabbergasted.

The disc jockey did two shows during the week on WNEW. *Collins on a Cloud* was a program of ballads and light jazz in the afternoon. As a harp played in the background, he had his listeners imagine that he was floating over the boroughs of New York.

"Hmmm, Jones Beach looks crowded today."

In his *Purple Grotto* at night, a piano played softly behind him as he rhapsodized between jazz records.

"Sarah Vaughn has made the grotto very purple tonight."

I thought both programs were the epitome of hip.

Saturday afternoons, Jazzbo played straight-ahead jazz by the big bands of Count Basie, Neil Hefti, Billy May and other swinging groups. He called the program *Man on the Beat* and I was going to see him do it.

Entering the lobby of WNEW, I spoke to the receptionist in my most grown-up voice.

"Dave Archard to see Mr. Collins." *Did Jazzbo really remember my name from the street?* She picked up her phone and pressed a button.

"That young man is here to see you," she said. Collins stuck his head out of an office and motioned for me to follow.

We walked the same hall where Martin Block, the King of Disc Jockeys, strolled, where Rayburn and Finch scampered down at dawn to do their wake-up show, and where Art Ford drifted in at midnight to preside over his *Milkman's Matinee*. Goose bumps crawled up my arms and over my shoulders.

Jazzbo went into the station's library with me behind. Single 45 rpm records in green paper sleeves and long-play albums in colorful covers leaned in partitions on metal shelves. He ignored the 45s, but went right to the LPs. After choosing albums, he surprised me by handing me the stack.

When he moved to larger discs of black and red, I knew what they were. My hard cover radio book had explained about electrical transcriptions or "ETs." Referring to a sheet, Jazzbo pulled the ones he needed. Looking at labels as they came out, I recognized the names Rayco Auto Seat Covers, Two Guys from Harrison and Robert Hall Clothes. *I know the words to those commercials and can sing the jingles.*

"Robert Hall this season will give you the reason. Low overhead. Low overhead."

Leaving the library, I walked side-by-side with Jazzbo, my arms weighted down with the albums, and we moved further down the hall. Entering a well-lit studio with gray and maroon walls, he waved at the engineer sitting in an upper-level control room and I placed the albums on a table, careful that none slid off.

Four cabinets with turntables and pick-up arms were positioned around a small podium on a seamless floor, and a microphone on a boom hung over the arrangement. To the left was a chair for me. There was no chair for Jazzbo Collins and I knew why.

Broadcasting-Telecasting magazine had published an interview with WNEW's program director, Bernice Judis. She insisted her personalities stand, not sit, to do their shows. That way, she figured, they wouldn't talk too much on the air.

"Do you operate your own turntables?" I asked.

"Sure do," Jazzbo answered, and as he waited to go on the air, he told me a story.

"When stations in the city switched over to playing records, their house bands were let go. Bigwigs at the musicians' union erupted. 'Our guys'll be reduced to playing for coins in the subway!' So a deal was struck. Union musicians became 'platter men,' setting-up turntables and releasing records by hand at signals by the DJs." He began to choose albums from the pile on the table. "Records were becoming free ads for recording companies," he continued, "especially the pop stuff Block was playing. The public demanded more, so recording studios sprang up over night.

Through negotiations, WNEW was able to get rid of those guys. Musicians have more work today than they can handle."

Jazzbo set up platters from albums on two turntables and his theme song on a third, but left the fourth one free for the commercials on ETs. At one o'clock, a voice came over a speaker from a DJ in a studio down the hall.

"That's it for me. Stay tuned for the man on the beat, 'Jazzbo' Collins. This is WNEW, New York."

Jazzbo started his theme, waited for it to establish, then asked for the air from the engineer by pointing at his microphone. A red light came on under the control room window, and he began his introduction. I realized he was being heard by millions of listeners in the tri-state area and, incredibly, I was there by his side.

As soon as he started the first LP, a telephone rang on the side of the table. Jazzbo picked up the receiver.

"Yes ma'am. No ma'am. Okay, ma'am," he said and hung up.

"Was that *Bernice Judis*?" I asked, my eyes wide.

"Yeah. She said I went too long on my intro." *Golly, Saturday afternoon, and the boss is listening.*

The man gave me a task to do while I watched him work. After playing a cut from the first LP, he slipped the platter back in its cover and slid the album over to me.

"Print the title and artist of the selections I play on that form on the table," he said, and handed me his pen. I felt important with my first honest-to-gosh assignment in radio.

Before half past the hour, a hefty man strolled into the studio and without saying a word, sat at a table in the corner. He turned on a lamp and pulled a desk mike toward him. Collins wrapped up the first part of his show, and Lonnie Starr gave his name and began reading five minutes of stories from the *New York Daily News. That's Lonnie Starr?* I heard him a hundred times on the station and was thrilled to be in the same room with the man.

Starr ended his newscast, and Jazzbo let loose with a surprise piece of music on a turntable. The jazz styling of Jackie Cain and Roy Kral cascaded from a wall speaker. My brother listened to records by the singer and her piano-playing husband often in our bedroom. The engineer in the control room bounced along in his chair to the music, a big smile on his face.

As I continued to write down the selections Jazzbo played, an album with a familiar cover came sliding over.

"Hey, 'Shorty Rogers Courts the Count.' My brother has this one!" I said. Jazzbo grinned.

When the show ended at two o'clock, he turned the reins over to Lonnie Starr, who had switched from news man to DJ in another studio. Before leaving, I thanked the paunchy man with the glasses and goatee.

"I'm getting into radio as soon as I get out of DJ school."

"Crazy," he said and shook my hand.

I retraced my steps along the hall where the legendary announcers of WNEW walked including Al "Jazzbo" Collins. Outside on Fifth Avenue, my feet barely touched the pavement as I drifted home on a cloud.

* * *

Guys stood apart from girls, and arms jiggled and hips gyrated as they danced to honking saxophones and deafening drum beats blasting from a 45 record changer. It was Christmas in 1955, and former classmates had returned from college and invited me to a party. I was surprised to find my friends had been pulled out of the safe cocoon of slow-dancing at Ridgewood High School and drawn into the big bad world of rock 'n' roll.

I read that "Moondog" was the moniker DJ Alan Freed used on the air in Cleveland. He shook up listeners along Lake Erie with the music my friends danced to that night in

Jersey. After he moved east to, of all places WNJR in Newark, WINS in New York hired him to shake, rattle and roll its audience in the Big Apple.

The newspaper article said the songs Freed played originated in the swamplands of the South. He kept his microphone open while a record was on to embellish the beat by slapping his hand on the Manhattan phone book. The new music on WINS was alien to sophisticated New York listeners, so I wanted to sample "Moondog" myself.

The music wasn't anything like the pop songs and jazz tunes I was used to hearing. The titles were strange like "Money Honey" and "Mend Your Ways," and singers' names like Clyde McPhatter and Ruth Brown were unfamiliar. When "Moondog" shouted between records, his voice was raw and guttural. *How different he sounds than the smooth guys on WNEW when they talk about Sinatra.* Listening to my radio as a kid in the forties, I lingered at the end of the dial to enjoy thumpin', bumpin' rhythm and blues coming from WWRL. In the fifties, I was intrigued with the raucous sound on WINS. *Will I play this kind of music when I get on the air?*

Alan Freed became wildly popular in New York by emceeing live theater shows throughout the five boroughs: If he didn't coin the term "rock 'n' roll," he sure capitalized on it.

* * *

"David, are you still interested in radio?" Mrs. Corbin was on the phone from the old neighborhood on the eastside.

"Uh-huh," I answered.

"Well, an announcer has moved in next door to us, and I thought you might like to meet him." An hour later, I was sipping a can of Pepsi in the man's living room.

Round, jolly, and bald, Johnny Clark told me he worked two jobs to support his wife and kids. Weeknights before midnight, he drove to the WOR towers between the oil refineries in Carteret, New Jersey. To save labor costs of an engineer in Manhattan, the one watching the transmitter in Jersey handled the controls for Johnny's graveyard shift of records. The second job was booth-announcing at Channel 9 on Saturdays.

"I'm going in this afternoon. Would you like to come with me?"

I accepted his offer in a heartbeat.

On the way to the city, I peppered Johnny Clark with questions about radio.

"How did you get started?" "What stations have you worked at?" "Do you like the music you play on WOR?" The smiling man answered with facts and quips as he negotiated through the traffic on Route 17.

Engrossed in our conversation, I forgot to look at the giant radio tower at Lodi as we sped by. After a run through the Lincoln Tunnel, we arrived in Manhattan, I shut up and the goose bumps began.

The studios and offices for WOR-TV Channel 9 were on Broadway, but master control, projection room, announce booth and transmitter were on Fifth Avenue and way up in the Empire State Building.

Johnny pulled into a parking lot on 39th Street and started off on foot with me tripping along beside him. I looked up at the antennas sticking out from a mast on the building's spire. At a thousand feet above the sidewalk, they radiated the signals of New York TV stations for miles in all directions including the rabbit ears in my bedroom.

We entered the lobby, a quiet elevator whooshed us up, and we stepped out on the eighty-third floor. As Johnny checked in to start his shift, I was drawn over to a wall of floor-to-ceiling windows.

The afternoon sky was light blue and cloudless. Gray and yellow roof tops of buildings stretched for blocks below to the Hudson River. I followed the dark blue water to my right until I saw the silver span of the George Washington Bridge glistening in the sun. Down to my left, I squinted at the green Statue of Liberty holding her torch high on a small island in the harbor. I looked across the river into the swamps of North Jersey and saw a plane take off like a flying ant from Teterboro Airport. Beyond, a patchwork quilt of highways and towns were laid out to the black humps of the Ramapo Mountains. I stood gaping until Johnny called to me: "Hey, Dave. C'mon."

We squeezed into a booth the size of a closet, and Johnny propped a copy book on a stand behind the microphone that hung on a short boom. He clamped a set of earphones on his head, pulled his chair up to the mike and cleared his throat.

A black-and-white movie played on the small screen in front of him. I recognized *The Belles of St. Trinian's*, a British comedy I'd seen on the station three or four times. A scene ended, the screen went black for a second, then lit up with a commercial film that showed the multiple uses of a salad chopper. When a slide followed, Johnny announced a Murray Hill 7 phone number and post office box to order the gadget.

He turned the page in the copy book, careful not to rattle the paper, and launched into an announcement for Dodger baseball while slides of batters and runners flashed on the screen. I sat quietly. *How many people are hearing him right now?* The movie started and Johnny sat back. A voice yelled over a talk-back speaker.

"What the hell was that, Clark?"

Johnny pushed a button and spoke into his mike.

"I'm just following the copy book."

I listened as the two men ironed out a glitch between audio and video. *I guess not everything goes smoothly in television.*

"That was the director in Master Control" Johnny said. "He and a bunch of technicians huddle there to put the breaks together. Besides me in the booth, they put on slides and films from the projection room. Live programs are brought in from the studios on Broadway and Dodger games from Ebbetts Field."

I threw out questions about the new medium I was seeing and Johnny fielded each one nicely. When he turned his chair toward the microphone for another break, I eased out to the hall.

Peeking in the next room, I discovered the station's movie projectors. One made a purring sound as *The Belles of St. Trinian's* ran through it. A technician threaded film through the sprockets of another. Other projectors stood in a line like silent sentinels, loaded with small reels of commercial film. I knew the projectors were an integral part of WOR-TV's programming. The station's *Million Dollar Movie* played the same Hollywood film at different times during the week. I could watch any showing of one and not miss *Sea Hunt* or *Highway Patrol* on the other channels.

Moving down the hall, I found the room I wanted. In the dim light of Master Control, three men hunched over a long desk of knobs and levers and stared at a bank of monitor screens.

The break in the movie started and a director on a tall chair behind them began a stream of commands. As I watched a monitor labeled AIR, slides and commercial film came on each time he spoke into a small, goose-neck microphone. When the director said "announce," Johnny's voice was heard. I realized that, unlike the way it worked in radio, Johnny couldn't see a cue through a slanted window, but instead was getting directions in his earphones. Although the men's fingers ran nimbly over the controls on the desk, their eyes never left the monitors. I shook my head. *I don't think I could handle this job. It's too nerve-wracking.*

Before returning to Johnny's booth, I entered a doorway at the end of the hall.

A row of grey steel cabinets stood side by side in a long, dimly lit room. Across the top of each were meters with needles quivering at different angles behind the glass. A cooling fan hummed, and the aroma in the room reminded me of the sweet smell in the control room at WPAT. Standing in front of Channel 9's mammoth transmitter, I marveled at the magic it took to send movies and ball games to the top of the Empire State Building and out to my TV set at home.

Johnny's shift ended, the next announcer went in the booth, and I walked over to the floor-to-ceiling windows to see how the view had changed. The sun was gone, leaving a thin streak of orange on the horizon. Headlights and tail lights formed strings of diamonds and rubies on the streets below, and lights were coming on in homes across the river in Jersey. My gaze was broken by Johnny's gentle nudge, and we headed to the elevators.

Wound-up by my exposure to television, I fired more questions about the other half of broadcasting as we rode home.

"How does film in a projector get on the air?" "How does a Dodger game come in from Ebbetts Field?" "Do the guys in Master Control get a break in their shift?" The jolly man behind the wheel answered patiently all the way back to Ridgewood.

Before jumping out of the car in his driveway, I shook Johnny's hand and thanked him for letting me tag along to Channel 9. Going home in the Plymouth, I went over everything I saw and heard and tried to file it away in my brain.

I would never forget that afternoon with Johnny Clark at the TV station in the sky with the magnificent view.

RIDING THE RAILS

Driving to the chemical factory, a question popped in my head. *If I'm going to the broadcasting school in Manhattan, wouldn't it make sense to get a job there, too?* Cash was stuffed to the rim of the "DJ School" jar with enough money to cover tuition. Working in the city would make it spill over. *I'll be rich!*

Sunday, I scoured the help wanted pages of the *Herald Tribune*. An ad for an employment agency said it placed people "in the exciting world of broadcasting." It was obvious these were jobs as errand boys and receptionists, but I'd experience the business first hand while training for it at the same time.

A problem arose.

Marge, our housekeeper, had moved into the house on Van Dyke Street and occupied a bedroom on the second floor. One day in the kitchen, I saw my father pull down her halter top. He laughed as she quickly pulled it up, but I was shocked. *Something's going on.*

It wasn't long before I heard the floor creak in the hall at night as Dad shuffled in slippers to Marge's room. After the door clicked shut, I put the pillow over my head to muffle the moans of ecstasy that followed. I knew what was happening and felt uneasy. Marge made my father happy, but she wasn't my mother. At age eighteen, I didn't think it was my place to say anything in the morning.

A single woman living in the same house with a widower raised eyebrows in Marge's small town of Midland Park. The Sunday she told Dad of being snubbed by the women at her Dutch Reform Church, he got mad.

"Those narrow-minded ol' biddies. Screw 'em!"

He bought a house further out in Bergen County, and we moved again.

* * *

The brand-new home was in a subdivision cut into the woods of Franklin Lakes, New Jersey. The one-story, ranch-style house stood on a dirt lot with plugs of grass planted in a checkerboard pattern. A driveway sloped into the one car garage under the house and a door opened from it into a full basement. Foil-wrapped duct work sprouted from the oil burner like thick silver limbs of a tree, but Dad had plenty of room to set up his workshop.

Upstairs, the kitchen was equipped with the latest range, oven and refrigerator. Dad even relented and bought a new-fangled dishwasher for Marge, but there was still no television set in the living room.

Down the hall were three bedrooms, two for the back-and-forth activity of father and housekeeper and a small one for me. I put the clunky TV set on the chest of drawers turned sideways at the foot of the bed. After I moved the rabbit ears around, a pretty good picture flickered on the screen. My radio worked fine.

The hardwood floors were shiny, and the whole place smelled of fresh paint, but the move to the house presented a dilemma. Stuck in the woods of Franklin Lakes, I was separated from the Erie Railroad miles away in Ridgewood. Because tolls and parking would eat up my budget, driving into Manhattan wasn't an option. Besides, the aging Plymouth wouldn't hold up for a daily run to and from the city, much less to the train station. I had to find a new way to commute.

I was unpacking books in my room – including the hard cover radio book – when I heard the sounds of a horn and the acceleration of an engine. *Could that be a train?* I hurried out the front door. The sounds came from the woods at the end of the subdivision.

Trotting down the street, I entered a thick stand of trees as the horn and engine began to fade. Running down a narrow path, I tripped on roots and rocks until the trees parted, and I skidded to a halt. In front of me was a train station!

A single set of rails ran by a boarded-up station house. Stepping on the cracked concrete platform, I walked along the front of the dilapidated building, its ticket window shut and padlocked. Inside a case decorated with spider webs on the wall, a faded timetable was pinned to a cork board. Through the dirty glass, I made out the schedule of days and times for trains.

The western route went deeper into North Jersey and turned up into the state of New York. The eastern route showed stops at towns I recognized from Bergen County to the Hudson River. Asterisks made me look down at connection times of buses that went through the Lincoln Tunnel to midtown Manhattan. *Hallelujah! I've been saved by the Susquehanna Railroad.*

* * *

The next morning, I picked out a tie from my collection of three to go with my one suit jacket and dipped into the "DJ School" jar for some cash. With money I'd saved, I was able to quit the job at Ultra Chemical and now regarded myself as a foot loose, fancy-free – although untrained and unemployed radio announcer. I whistled as I strolled through the trees to the new-found train station.

I was first to arrive on the platform. A horn sounded up the line in Oakland and people in business attire appeared out of the woods. A silver engine leaning on the rails rounded a bend, a row of ice-blue windows wrapped around its blunt nose. I heard a squeal, but no hiss of steam as the train glided in and stopped. A diesel motor purred inside the polished body of the engine as I stepped in the first of five shiny passenger cars.

I made my way along a spotless red floor to a window seat. The plush leather cushion gave a sigh as I sat. The tan rubber on the arm rests felt soft and smooth.

How different this is than the sooty old Erie Pullman with hard benches I rode as a kid.

A conductor in a crisp blue uniform and smart billed cap came down the aisle and sold me a ticket. As the train moved away from the platform, I settled in my seat and looked out a squeaky-clean window.

The woods of Franklin Lakes gave way to the backs of buildings in Wyckoff where other passengers got on. When the hills of Midland Park came into view, more riders climbed aboard. The train made a wide turn and ignored Ridgewood all together. After a stop at Hawthorne, it picked up speed, dove under the Erie tracks and dashed through the reeds of the Jersey swamps to make its final stop under a bridge in Secaucus.

Everyone on my car got off, so I followed and climbed aboard a black and white bus idling nearby. We jostled together on the highway of pot holes that cut into the granite of the Palisades and under the apartment where my aunt and uncle lived in Union City. The bus caught up to other traffic and started the slow crawl around the curve to the mouth of the Lincoln Tunnel.

After a smelly ride under the river, the bus emerged in the bright morning sun. I had arrived at the destination of my fate, "The Big Apple," "Baghdad on the Hudson," "The City That Never Sleeps." Beneath the Port Authority Bus Terminal, a subway could take me to wherever a job was waiting in that wonderful city.

I found the employment agency in midtown and after listing my limited qualifications, was sent to a job interview. It was for the position of production assistant at Barry-Enright Productions.

From an article in *B-T* magazine, I'd learned the company produced popular quiz shows for the TV networks. *How great would that be? Getting coffee for the director, rubbing elbows with the crew, being right on the floor while a show was on the air!* The Personnel Director at Barry-Enright scanned my application through glasses perched on her nose. When she saw I lived beyond normal commuter towns in North Jersey, she frowned.

"This position requires late hours at the studios. You wouldn't have connections left to get home at night." I didn't get the job. Probably some guy from the Bronx with only a subway ride home was hired. *What the heck, I'm going to a DJ school at night anyway.*

* * *

Returning to the city the next morning for another try with the employment agency, I couldn't resist the temptation to do something else first. I got off the bus at the Port Authority terminal and ran down to a row of phone booths on the main floor. Flipping the pages of a heavy Manhattan phone book, I found the address I wanted then hurried out into the morning sun because I knew at that very moment Bob and Ray were on the air at WINS. My steps quickened along 42nd Street.

It was ten minutes to nine when I reached the office building for the station. The glass doors to the lobby were unlocked. No one was in there to challenge me. An empty unmanned elevator waited with its doors open. I entered it and pressed the button for "WINS Studios." Arriving on the floor, I walked down a deserted hallway to a glowing On Air light. I looked in the small window of a door, and there they were.

With jackets off and sleeves rolled up, Bob and Ray sat side by side under two boom mikes. Their desk was strewn with paper, coffee cups were pushed aside. Balding Bob talked as heavy-set Ray nodded. My stomach flipped to be so close to the pair, better than seeing them from afar at Radio City. *Dare I go in?* I backed away.

Moving to the door of an adjoining studio, I recognized the man seated in there from his photo in the *Sunday Radio Guide*. With dark framed glasses above a bushy moustache, Peter Roberts prepared to go on the air with the news.

Besides his distinctive voice heard on movie newsreels, Roberts had an extraordinary laugh. At least once each morning, Bob and Ray made the man burst out laughing at the end of a newscast. I only imagined what they did on their side of the slanted window to get him started. Peter Roberts' laughter would continue between gasps for air and groans of "Oh, no." The pair let him go on every time without saying a word.

The red light went off at Bob and Ray's studio. I went back to their door and hesitated. Security was lax – no one was in the hallway to stop me – but I pulled my hand back from the handle. I turned and walked to the elevator.

Out on the street, I slapped my hip. *Damn it. I could have gone in, shook their hands and told Bob and Ray how much I liked them. I had no trouble introducing myself to Jazzbo. Why couldn't I have done the same with them?* I walked to the employment agency, disgusted with myself and my terrible lack of nerve.

* * *

I was sent uptown for an opening at a big radio-television company. The waiting room in the personnel department was crowded. Young men and women sat on hard plastic chairs and stared ahead, hoping for a job "in the exciting world of broadcasting."

A secretary gave me an application form, said to fill it out, and wait for my name to be called. I began writing until the lines for "work history" stopped me. I pondered how the jobs at the A & P, dental lab and chemical factory would look, but I wrote them down anyway. At least it showed I was employable and could hold a job.

Others in the room were called one by one to be interviewed. Sitting rigid, I drummed my fingers on my knees. *I hope there's a job left for me.* Finally, a man stepped in from a hall and called my name.

"David Arc-hard?" I stood and followed him to a cubicle office space. He glanced at my application, laid it down and hit it with a rubber stamp.

"You're hired," he said, and I jumped.

He explained what my job would be and that I was to start the following Monday.

A creepy little guy appeared and took me on a confusing route through hallways and past offices to show me where I was to work. His voice cracked when he spoke. "Good luck."

Outside, my feet barely touched the sidewalk. On the train home, I picked out in my mind which tie I was going to wear on my first day at the American Broadcasting Company.

THE ABC OF RADIO AND TELEVISION

How exhilarating to walk into the lobby at 7 West 66th Street. I smiled and snapped a sharp salute to the attractive woman in the trim uniform at the reception desk. Passing the long slanted window of Master Control, I waved at the engineer inside. Setting a jaunty pace down a pale blue hall, I glanced into open doors of studios, each one lit with a warm glow. At the end, a red On Air light flashed beside a closed door. *I wonder what's was going on in there.* Reaching my destination, I marched smartly down a ramp and entered the noisy, smelly mail room in the basement of ABC.

Young men in white shirts and ties sorted letters and packages from a hamper on wheels. They looked at each piece then placed it in the proper wooden cubicle. Others stuffed mail wrapped with rubber bands into leather bags and started out on foot. I watched as a guy inserted envelopes in a squat metal box. They shot out the other end in rapid succession with postage printed on them.

In the next room where I was to work, guys in plaid shirts and dark pants hunched over mimeograph machines. Smudged paper littered the floor. The smell of printer's ink filled the air. A short man wearing a black rubber apron from his chest to his knees, called me over.

"You Archard?"

"Yeah."

"I'm Joe, the manager." He shook my hand and without wasting a second, launched into his instructions.

"Blue stencils come down over there from Central Typing upstairs."

"Over there" was a box on a rope inside a shaft. Contraptions like that called "dumb waiters" sent meals up from basement kitchens to dining rooms in ritzy apartments on Park Avenue. At ABC, it worked in reverse. Typists lowered the box filled with work, and it was sent back up when empty.

"Get me a stencil from the box and bring it here," Joe said.

I did and he clamped it on the drum of a mimeograph machine and loaded it with the paper indicated on a work order. I tried to follow his quick movements. He turned the drum by hand, and paper slid out on a tray.

"Words too light? Too dark?" He adjusted the ink flow accordingly.

Turning small numbered wheels with his thumb, he set the count for the required copies and switched on the motor. The drum rotated, and the first page of a soap opera script began to print.

"That's what you do," Joe said and he walked away.

Bewildered, I scratched my head while the machine whirred and clicked. I tried to remember ink flow, copy count and switch. Copies of page one of the soap opera script continued to fly out and land in a tray. I picked one up and read the title. *Hey, Whispering Streets!*

After I got the hang of running the mimeograph machine, the job wasn't difficult. A little messy, but the pink glop from a jar in the washroom took the black off my hands at the end of the day. The best thing about the job was that I got to read every script, sales piece and press release that came out of the machine.

A mixed bunch of guys worked in the basement of ABC. The ones who paraded past me with their noses in the air and their little leather shoulder bags filled with mail were aspiring actors and directors waiting for their big break. None of the ones in the mimeograph room with me professed to want a future in broadcasting. They were there because it was a job. I regarded my employment as a terrific opportunity. On coffee breaks and at lunch, I could roam the halls of ABC to check out any studio I wanted without asking to be let in.

* * *

Headquartered a half-block in from Central Park on West 66th, the American Broadcasting Company combined local WABC Radio and Channel 7 with its network radio and television operations. Three old buildings jammed together were accessible to each other through doorways busted through the walls. The mimeo operator next to me said there had been a riding academy in one building before ABC converted it to a big TV studio.

"The smell of manure in this place is from either past horses or current management upstairs," he said with a twisted grin on his face.

Starting self-guided tours of the three buildings, I was drawn first to the Radio Division. Master control for the network was visible to the public through a long slanted window in the lobby. An engineer sat at a massive control board built in to a custom-made blue Formica counter. Programs from studios throughout the building came into the room at the appropriate time and were sent out on phone lines to hundreds of stations across the country. I stood and stared.

On a break one morning, I peeked around the open door of a studio and saw the cast of *When a Girl Marries* waiting to go on the air. Actors and actresses for the soap opera slouched around floor mikes with scripts hanging loosely at their sides. *Do they realize their days on the program are numbered?* Television was ending the "Golden Age of Radio." The new way to communicate in 1955 was to the eye as well as the ear. Imagination on the airwaves was dying.

* * *

I thought it was a big deal to sit on a plush seat of a clients' booth in the TV division. All I needed to look like a sponsor was a cigar in one hand, a glass of Scotch in the other, and thirty years tacked on my life.

Down in the studio, a thousand things were happening at once. Two young men rehearsed a skit; musicians and a girl singer lounged around a piano; three cameramen fiddled with their cameras. On a ladder, one man adjusted lights. On the floor, another spoke into a small mike attached to his earphones. I saw a woman holding a powder puff from a makeup kit while another wrote with a black marker on a large white card. A man standing atop a platform on rubber tires kept swinging a boom mike back and forth over this activity. Although I understood most of what was going on, I didn't know who the two young men in the skit were.

"Who are they? From nightclubs? Broadway?" I asked out loud.

A typist on her break in back of me spoke up.

"They're Peter Marshall and Tommy Noonan, but that's all I know."

Women carrying shopping bags filed in and sat on folding chairs at the edge of the set. The cast and crew continued their busy work until a half hour of comedy and music came together at noon on Channel 7.

* * *

At lunch time, guys from the mail room and girls from central typing crowded into a delicatessen a few doors away from ABC. It was there Charlie Heinz introduced me to yogurt.

Charlie ran the mimeograph machine across the aisle from me. He lived in Oradell, New Jersey, played piano in a band on weekends and said he knew my brother.

If the weather was pleasant, we took our brown bags to a bench in Central Park and ate with the squirrels. After a pastrami on rye, cream soda and cup of Dannon one afternoon, Charlie and I went back to ABC to play at radio.

We found an empty studio, looked up and down the hall, then snuck in. Heinz went to the piano in a corner, and I sat under a boom mike. His jazzy riffs on the keyboard punctuated my babbling as a beatnik poet.

"Dead. The day hung dead. A meaningless rag wiped the sullen moon and a melting clock beat time to the waving corn. Oh, the depths of mediocrity overshadowed the shine of the drain and above it all, a wilted basket overflowed with the sand of my soul."

A janitor with a mop and pail pushed open the studio door, but bowed and backed out. He thought he was interrupting a broadcast.

* * *

Dramas, comedies and quiz shows were disappearing from network radio, but ABC made an effort to keep live music on the air. One program featured the solo talent of an orchestra leader from the big band era. Bobby Sherwood was also a piano player, singer and pretty funny guy. He sat at the keyboard for an hour in the afternoon and played, sang and did comedy bits.

I listened to him when I drove for the dental lab and my appreciation grew for the meaningful lyrics that went with the wonderful melodies of the songs he sang: "In the Still Of

The Night," "All The Things You Are," "I Get Along Without You Very Well" to name a few. Sherwood said the songs were written in the 30s and 40s by Cole Porter, Jerome Kern, Hoagy Carmichael, Rodgers and Hart, Irving Berlin, Johnny Mercer and a whole host of other composers.

"Their songs are called 'standards'," he said one afternoon, "because they fit the rules that all music is measured by in our culture, and they'll live forever." I decided then that was the music I wanted to play when I got on the air.

Bobby Sherwood was gone from the halls of ABC soon after I started at the company, so I never found him. He was taken off the air to make way for a famous disc jockey and a program of recorded pop music.

BLOCK AND ERNIE

Martin Block was a giant in New York. As host of *The Make Believe Ballroom* on WNEW, he was the most listened-to disc jockey in the market. Record promoters flocked to him to have their products introduced by his syrupy patter in a baritone voice. The American Broadcasting Company figured he could be big across the country, so it hired the man to host three hours of records in the afternoon on its radio network.

According to my *B-T* magazine, Martin Block was wooed away from WNEW by a large salary and his own studio. On the top floor of the radio division, ABC redecorated and refurnished a studio especially for his show. One afternoon during my break, I rode an elevator from the mimeograph room to see it and him.

In the control room, I stood next to the show's producer and an engineer seated at his elbow. Through the slanted window, I watched a union platter man operate turntables in the corner of the studio. While a record played, a young woman leaned over a slight man seated at a microphone on a boom and handed him papers. Because of the small moustache and receding hairline I'd seen in one of his photos, I knew he was Martin Block.

Seated in a high-backed chair at an over-sized desk, he looked like a king holding court. He didn't look happy. Even though he was paid royally to come over to ABC, I wondered if he was sorry he left the comfortable *Make Believe Ballroom* at less-stressful WNEW.

* * *

Ernie Kovacs and I worked in the same building at ABC. While I slaved all day in the mimeograph room, the comedic legend had fun in the morning in the radio division.

If I hurried below the bus terminal and caught the right subway uptown, I arrived at ABC in time to watch Kovacs from the control room before he went off at 9 a.m. I knew I'd made it in time if I saw his limousine parked in front of 7 West 66th, the chauffer slumped behind the wheel reading a newspaper.

I read that Kovacs began as a disc jockey in Trenton, New Jersey before moving to Philadelphia to host a wacky local TV show. His imaginative stunts and rubbery face caught the eye of Dumont Television. He was brought to New York and given a daytime program on the network's station, Channel 5. Whenever I watched him on TV, I got a kick out of his visual bits. He'd peer through a car tire hanging on a rope and blow cigar smoke at the camera, or he'd wear plastic bug eyes and recite poetry as lisping "Percy Dovetonsils."

Kovacs' morning show on WABC was a big production even for New York radio. Besides a five-piece band, the station assigned ABC's senior sound effects man to it. While Kovacs performed skits with silly names and voices, I watched Keene Crocket work with his pile of toys in the back of the studio to create door slams, gun shots and fog horn blasts.

As the band played its final number in the radio studio one morning, Kovacs stood up, pulled the shirttail out of his fly and waved it around in front of the musicians.

They didn't break, but I laughed. When he came into the control room to confer with the engineer, he glanced over at me.

"Hey, kid," he said.

I nodded without saying a word then floated down to the mimeograph room to start my shift.

* * *

If I kept my eyes open at ABC, I saw other people in the broadcast business.

A short man in a suit came running into the mimeograph room once to check on a project we were churning out. Because I read *Broadcasting-Telecasting* from cover to cover every week, I recognized him – a rising young executive at ABC many new ideas for the television network. Impressed that he left his suite upstairs and came down to our messy room, I nudged the guy next to me and whispered. "That's Don Durgan!"

He shrugged. "So?"

Alone on a break one afternoon, I was buying a Butterfinger from the candy machine in a hall when a woman approached from the TV studios. As she got closer, I recognized popular singer Giselle McKenzie.

"Could you tell me where the ladies' room is?" she said.

I pointed and held a door open for her.

"Thank yew," she said sweetly as she breezed by.

The company Christmas party in 1955 was held after work in the large TV studio, the one with the supposed smell of horses. Charlie, Joe and I stood elbow-to-elbow with other employees, clients and celebrities to enjoy food, booze and a band.

Ernie Kovacs, the emcee, asked a burly man with a bulldog face to come up on stage. The man stepped to the microphone to thank us for another wonderful year. Most of the people in the room didn't know who he was until Kovacs introduced him, but I recognized the president of ABC, Robert Kintner, the moment I saw him.

* * *

When it was my turn to be the stand-by mimeograph operator one Sunday afternoon, I arrived in the deserted mail room at 3:30 p.m. and stood by my machine. Before quitting time Friday, our manager, Joe, had told me what to expect on the Sunday shift. He said the box in the shaft might thump down at any time with a special job.

"After rehearsal for *The Greatest Story Ever Told*, some editing of the script is a possibility. You gotta be ready to run off the revisions."

He explained that a girl would be waiting upstairs in central typing to retype any pages marked with scribbled notes and cross-outs by the director. She'd send the new stencils down to me to be printed and collated before a production assistant came by to pick up the revised work.

"If nothing comes down by four o'clock," he said, "go home."

Wow, I'll be part of a radio show!

The Greatest Story Ever Told was a dramatization of Bible stories sent out on the network at 5:30 p.m. The elaborate production required the biggest studio in the radio division to accommodate a bevy of actors, a chorus of singers and an orchestra filled with strings and French horns. A team of three sound effects men were needed to recreate hoof beats and chariot wheels on the ancient roads of the Holy Land. After rehearsal, some words could be revised and others deleted for timing – and the new script depended on the girl upstairs and me. I waited at my machine and felt very important.

At four o'clock, the box in the shaft didn't thump. I waited until 4:15. No stencils came down. After turning off the lights, I walked up the ramp to the hall of studios, but instead of leaving the building, I was tempted to take another self-guided tour of ABC.

Entering a control room in the Radio Division, I nodded to the engineer and looked through the slanted window in front of him to see what was going on. In a studio no bigger than my bedroom at Dad's house, an announcer sat slumped in a chair under a boom mike. His tie was loosened, his collar unbuttoned, his hair mussed. He was waiting to go on the air with another edition of a program he'd been announcing every hour since noon.

It's Time, a five-minute news-behind-the-news feature sponsored by TIME magazine, required the announcer to deliver the program in the same shouted style of Westbrook Van Voorhis, the narrator on *The March of Time* newsreels at the movies. The announcer's full energy was needed to put the program across to the listeners.

As the clock hands moved toward 4:25, he straightened up and shook his head from side to side. The engineer started blaring theme music on the control room turntable and threw him a finger cue. The announcer started by shouting.

"It's TIME!"

He reported on the Big Four meeting in Geneva and the death of Albert Einstein, his voice strident, his delivery rapid. He gripped the script with one hand, pumped the fist of the other, and his face became red. His voice never weakened as he read a profile of Chuck Berry, already a top recording artist on both pop and rhythm and blues charts.

The announcer didn't even slow down at the end when he delivered a commercial for TIME magazine. *Did he go through the entire five minutes without taking a breath?*

When he finished, the theme music played again. He looked at the clock and had just enough oomph left to give the necessary sign-off.

"This is ABC, the American Broadcasting Company."

Exhausted, the announcer leaned back in his chair, looked at the ceiling and took a deep breath. *I hope that's not an announcing job I'll have to do.* I didn't realize then that I'd be one of the on-air participants in the rapid-fire Top Forty record format that was bubbling under the radio business.

* * *

One morning in January, Joe tacked a memo on the bulletin board, and mimeo operators gathered around to read it. It showed the date and time for open auditions for the radio network. Not only were the auditions available for professional actors and announcers, they were open for all ABC employees – office workers, secretaries, technicians and us. The guys snickered.

"Sure, management thinks there's talent down here," said one.

"Or delivering mail upstairs," said a second.

"Or goofing off at the snack machine like Archard," said a third.

We all laughed, but secretly I thought it was a nice gesture by the company – and maybe I could learn something by auditioning.

When the day came, I told Joe in a loud voice that I was going on a break. I strolled from the room, and once out of sight, ran up the ramp. Walking down the hall of studios, my legs became rubbery. *Do I really want to do this?*

I joined two men leaning against a wall at the assigned studio. Both were older and wore suits. One took a final puff of a cigarette and snuffed it out in a container of sand. The other glanced at his watch and frowned. *Do they work here at ABC or are they from somewhere else?*

A bored-looking secretary at the studio door asked my name and handed me two news stories and a piece of commercial copy.

"Read these over and be ready when your name is called," she said flatly. I glanced at the material, but didn't mark anything – a mistake. I mouthed the words so no one in the hall could hear me – another mistake. Before I could look at them again, the secretary called out.

"Archard, these men have already auditioned. You're up."

I entered a darkened studio. Unlike the other studios, there was no warm glow – only one section of lights in the ceiling lit a bare table and one chair. The place looked like the interrogation room in a police movie.

I sat and stared at the microphone hanging from a boom in front of my face.

Four stark-white panels surrounded the square base of the mike with simple block letters in black: A B C. A rush of excitement went through me. *I'm going to speak into an actual "hot" network microphone.*

A voice jolted me. "Whenever you're ready."

I looked in the control room. A man seated behind the slanted window had spoken over a speaker mike. *Gee, maybe he's a director searching for a just-right voice to play a part on one of the few remaining dramas on the network.*

I moistened my lips with my tongue. *Too late for a cup of water.* I read the news stories and commercial, hoping I wouldn't choke. Finishing, I relaxed in the chair. The man's voice over the speaker was gentle.

"Because you have a light voice, you need to put more inflection in your delivery. Use a pencil and underline the action words in your copy, then practice them by reading out loud. Good luck. Next!"

BROADCASTING 101

With my savings from working in Jersey and the job at ABC, I was ready to begin my training to be a disc jockey. Each week, the half-page ad in *B-T* magazine for the Columbia School of Broadcasting intimidated me. "Extensive faculty" implied I might be lost before a number of instructors in a multitude of classrooms. "Modern facility" and "latest equipment" made it sound expensive.

I found another ad for a school tucked in the classified section of the Sunday *Herald Tribune*. Because it was only a column wide and two inches deep, I figured the school was smaller. *I'll get individual attention, and it's probably cheaper.* I chose Broadcast Coaching Associates.

BCA was on the fourth floor of an old building at Broadway and 53rd Street. Walking down a dark hall from a creaky elevator, I entered the school's tiny office. A cheery secretary in a simple blouse and skirt welcomed me and handed me an enrollment form.

"The course runs sixteen weeks, and the cost is broken into weekly payments. I'll collect them every Tuesday before class," she said. *What? No tuition in advance?* I happily counted out fifty dollars from a wad of bills and put the rest back in my pocket.

As the secretary wrote a receipt, thoughts flooded my brain. *Was the past year wasted? Did I have to endure the dumb jobs in Jersey? Could I have worked at ABC right after high school and come here sooner?* I shook them from my head as she directed me to the next room.

Walking out on the worn floor of a rehearsal hall for dancers, I saw my reflection in a floor-to-ceiling mirror and automatically smoothed my hair. A waist-high warm-up bar ran along the mirror, but I resisted the silly urge to hike my leg up on it like a ballet dancer, afraid my pants would rip. I ran my fingers down the chipped keys of a scarred upright piano in the corner, and the notes that came out sounded tinny. In the middle of the room, metal folding chairs were arranged in front of a backboard on wheels. *I guess this is also the classroom for the DJ school.*

Peering into an adjoining room a little bigger than a closet, my heart sank. A stubby control board with knobs the size of thimbles sat on a plain wooden table with spindly legs. A record player with flocked turntable and curved pick-up arm looked like something a teenaged girl would receive as a birthday gift. The bulbous microphone on a desk stand was the type used by police departments for "calling all cars." Compared to the professional control rooms I was seeing at ABC, the make-believe one at BCA was pathetic. Still, I was eager to get my hands on everything in there.

Other people wandered into the rehearsal hall. I joined them on a row of folding chairs and leaned over.

"Hi, I'm Dave."

A guy with a withered left arm hanging from his shirt sleeve mumbled. "I'm Sal from Brooklyn."

An older Negro woman placed a big cloth bag on the floor and nodded to me.

"Hello. My name is Pearl."

I wonder if these two have any chance at becoming DJs.

A busty girl next to me put her hand on my knee.

"My name is Tammy. I'm also taking lessons in this building to sing on Broadway. Where are you from?"

My gaze at the curves in her sweater was interrupted as three men in suits strode into the room. The faculty for Broadcast Coaching Associates stood shoulder to shoulder before us.

The first instructor stepped forward. He had a small moustache, wore horn-rimmed glasses and spoke in a mellow voice.

"I'm Fred Darwin, the director of the school and I'm an announcer at WPAT in Paterson over in Jersey." *Hey, my old friend WPAT!*

The next one, short with sandy hair, spoke.

"I'm Bill Maher. I'm on the announcing staff at WOR and handle assignments for the Mutual network." *Whoa, prestigious WOR and Mutual!*

A tall, olive-skinned man stood erect and put his big hands in back of him.

"My name is Ernie Althschuler. I'm a studio engineer at CBS Radio, and I helped develop a reverberation device that juices up the music on the network." *CBS! I wonder if he knows Arthur Godfrey. I can't wait to learn from these men.*

Fred Darwin gave us the hard facts right off.

"You won't start in the radio business here in New York. This is where you'll end up if you want to. It's taken years for the three of us to get here. You'll begin at a station somewhere else and do everything. I mean, operate the controls, play records, rip news off the teletype, take transmitter readings, answer the phone, sweep the floor and – oh yeah – announce." We all laughed.

"Your first job is not guaranteed when you finish the course here," he went on. "However, we'll give you leads to stations that have submitted openings to us." It didn't take much for me to figure they were small stations in small towns that couldn't afford experienced announcers and had to take chances with beginners. *I don't care where I start. I want to get on the air as soon as I can.*

Two-hour classes started at 7 p.m. on Tuesday, Wednesday and Thursday. At the end of the first session, I checked my watch. There was just enough time to get to the Port Authority Bus Terminal and catch a black-and-white out to the train in the swamps. *How terrible if I miss the last run of the day on the Susquehanna.* I said a hasty goodnight to my new classmates, the creaky elevator dropped me to 53rd Street, and I bolted out the door.

Running west, I realized a stop-and-go bus on Eighth Avenue would be too slow. Turning south on Eighth, I rushed past delis, pawn shops and vegetable stands, dodging people coming the other way. I looked ahead to traffic lights at side streets and judged if I could make it across before they changed. When I could, I leaped off the sidewalk and dashed in front of waiting taxis and buses. If I saw I couldn't, I put on the brakes at the edge of the curb.

As my arms and legs pumped, I remembered running the mile on the track team in high school. My spikes let me fly on the cinders then, but the loafers I was wearing made me slip and slide on the sidewalks of Eighth Avenue. Holding both arms out for balance, I danced down the remaining blocks to 43rd Street.

Arriving at the terminal, I took stairs two at a time to the buses for Jersey, jumped on the one I needed and flopped in a seat. The bus started out, ducked down a ramp and dove into the Lincoln Tunnel. *If this bus isn't fast enough, I'll have to spend the night under the bridge at Secaucus.* As it pulled up to the platform in the swamps, I let out a sigh. The train was waiting, its engine purring.

I sprawled on a seat in an empty passenger car and caught my breath. As the train began to move, the bare truth smacked me. I would have to run down Eighth Avenue three times a week for the next sixteen weeks.

Through Slanted Windows

* * *

In the first week at the broadcasting school, Bill Maher had the class do something odd.

"You need to loosen the muscles in your face to help you enunciate better. Everyone, get on your feet," he commanded. He walked in front of us like a drill sergeant in the Marines.

"You're going to say the vowels in the alphabet out loud, but with great exaggeration." He stopped and faced us.

"Pull your lips back on 'A.' Put your teeth together on 'E.' Open your mouth wide for 'I.' Form a big 'O' with your lips and purse them together to make the 'U.' Okay, now try it." I felt silly, but if the exercise helped Maher get to WOR, I did what he said.

Next, the instructor had each of us stand up and deliver a sign-off to a dance band remote broadcast. I didn't understand why.

"That's not something we'll have to do at a small station in Podunk," I said.

He glared at me.

"It will develop your ability to talk extemporaneously or 'ad lib' without a script in whatever on-air situation you might be in."

"Oh," I said sheepishly.

Maher jotted the elements on the blackboard to be included in the sign-off, but not in the order he wrote them.

"Work those lines around so they make sense."

When it was my turn, the assignment was a snap.

"From the beautiful ballroom of the Hotel Edison in downtown Times Square, New York, you've been listening to the scintillating rhythms of Henry Jerome and his orchestra, brought to you by the Air National Guard. Dave Archard speaking. This is Mutual, the Radio Network for All America."

I had added the words "beautiful," "downtown Times Square," and "the scintillating rhythms of" to Maher's words on the blackboard. I sat down with a smug expression.

* * *

A week later, Fred Darwin punctured my ego. He had me read a story from news copy he brought in from the teletype machine at WPAT.

"Police were called to the Adams Pharmacy on Amsterdam Avenue in Harlem after it was broken into last night. Thousands of dollars of narcotics were stolen. Authorities are looking for two men who were seen leaving the drug store shortly after midnight."

When I finished, Darwin pointed out some sloppiness in my speech.

"You pronounced 'police' as 'pleese,' and the 'drug' in 'drug store' came out with too hard a 'd'." I was shocked. Although raised in the affluent suburbs of Bergen County where everyone spoke with perfect diction, I didn't realize some "Jersey-ese" had crept into my mine. I sat down deflated. *Have I come all this way to find I have an accent?*

After everyone in the class read their news stories, Darwin made me deliver mine again. I pronounced each word with care, especially "police" and "drug" store.

"Much better," he said.

* * *

At last the time came to touch the simple equipment in the make-believe control room. The class crowded around the door of the closet-sized room. Ernie Althschuler had each student sit at the small control board to get the feel of handling the turntable, flipping the switches and talking into the mike.

When he motioned for me to come in, I strolled in with chest out. I sat, pulled myself up to the control board and put on earphones. He handed me a 45 record, "Tumbling Tumble Weeds" by Gene Autry. Cueing the record on the turntable, I turned on the mike switch with a swipe of a finger and sailed into my intro with great bravado.

When I started the turntable, the pick-up arm slipped off the edge of the record!

Looking out of the corner of my eye, I reached over and placed the needle on the first groove while I filled with a stupendous ad lib.

"Gene Autry was the star of cowboy movies in the forties. Today, he's a successful business man in California and owns several radio stations out west. Now, here's Gene..." Going to Saturday matinees as a kid and reading *Broadcasting-Telecasting* cover to cover saved me on that exercise.

As class wrapped up for the evening, Althschuler pulled me aside.

"You seem smart enough," he said. "Why don't you get a third-class license before you leave here? The other students will mail a form to the FCC for a restricted ticket. They'd get back a wallet-size card that allows cab drivers, truck dispatchers and mere disc jockeys to operate non-directional transmitters. With a third-class license, you'll be able to operate more sophisticated ones. It'll impress station managers that you're a serious broadcaster." I nodded that I understood, so he handed me a thick book to study.

At home, I opened the book to the first chapter and was immediately mystified by the technical jargon as I had been with the hard cover radio book. Slogging through the material, I struggled with terms like "signal patterns" and "frequency strength," often going back to read and reread hard-to-understand paragraphs.

A week later, I was in a cold, cavernous room at the Federal Building in lower Manhattan. Seated with other aspiring broadcasters at a row of tables, I fiddled with the exam booklet. When the command was given to begin, I opened the cover. *Hey, multiple choice answers.* Relaxing, I lowered my head and put the pencil to work.

A manila envelope arrived at Dad's house in Franklin Lakes a month later. Official-looking printing on the outside told me it was from the Federal Communications Commission, Washington, D.C. I pulled out an 8-by-10 blue document and read the heading, "Third Class Radiotelephone License." *I'm a damn engineer!* I framed the document and put it with the other things I wanted to take to my first job in radio.

* * *

One evening at the DJ school, Bill Maher wrote the word "resume" on the blackboard and added an accent mark above the last 'e.'

"That word's pronounced 'rez-a-may,'" he said. "It's to be a single page about yourself to send with your audition tape when applying to a station."

He wrote the elements on the blackboard of a "rez-a-may" and told the class to get busy writing our own.

At the top of the page, I printed my name and the address and phone number of Dad's house. Stuff like age, sex and marital status went on the next five lines.

Education followed. Under "Ridgewood High School, Ridgewood, N.J.," I added "Broadcast Coaching Associates, New York, N.Y."

Work experience was next. I worried about what to include as I had when I filled out the job application at ABC. *"Assembly announcer in high school?" Nah, too immature.* I left off the A & P, dental lab and chemical factory, but put down "printing technician at the American Broadcasting Company, New York, N.Y." I cringed, but it was better than "mimeograph operator." *Including ABC should mean something, too.*

At the bottom of the page, I had to list references. Without hesitating, I printed the names of the three instructors at BCA, including their affiliation with WPAT, WOR and CBS Radio. *Now that means something.*

Maher gave us all a suggestion. "A small head-and-shoulder photo of you in the upper right-hand corner will help." At home that night, I found the proof sheet of poses I'd kept for my high school yearbook picture and cut one out.

The following Saturday, I went to a printer in Ridgewood with the information and photo in hand. Within a week, a fine set of two dozen "rez-a-mays" rolled off the press. *I wonder how many I'll have to send to get my first job in radio?*

SNEAKING IN ON ARTHUR

Work in the mimeograph room at ABC ended at five o'clock. Class at school didn't start until seven, so I had plenty of time to take a bus down from 66th Street and grab a cheap dinner in Times Square. After enjoying a hot dog and orange drink at Nedick's, I sauntered up Broadway.

At the Brill Building, I stopped and lingered. According to my brother's *Downbeat*, famous singers and songwriters had offices on floors above, but I recognized no one coming out of the gold doors on the street.

Further along, a shiny theater marquee announced *Mr. Wonderful Starring Sammy Davis, Jr.* I looked around the corner to maybe catch Sammy going in the stage door, but only people rushed by to catch subways home.

As I walked, I dreamed. *I'll come back to this magnificent city some day and walk this street as a celebrity.*

An old theater on Broadway between 53rd and 54th was crammed between two office buildings, one of them with the creaky elevator and my broadcasting school. Large white letters on a black background ran down a three-story vertical sign on the front of the theater and they excited me every time I looked up at them.

C
B
S

T
E
L
E
V
I
S
I
O
N

 I knew that people sat in there Sundays to see Ed Sullivan introduce dog acts and plate spinners. On Wednesdays, crowds enjoyed the little Godfreys performing under the watchful eye of Arthur. Saturdays, audiences howled as Jackie Gleason dominated the stage as Joe the Bartender, Ralph Cramden and the Poor Soul. Week after week, their programs went out to millions of viewers across America, including me in Ridgewood.

 Watching the programs on my bedroom TV, I always pictured what the crews looked like pushing cameras and swinging boom mikes during the broadcasts, but peering through the ornate doors of iron and glass at the theater on Broadway, I saw nothing in the dark lobby.

 One spring evening, I ended my after-dinner stroll at the CBS Theater and wandered down 53rd Street. Noticing a side door open, I ran up to it and stopped. A folding gate blocked the entrance. Through the openings, I saw men wearing tool belts and pushing trellises entwined with greenery across a stage. The sound of a band playing drifted out to the street. *It's Wednesday, so that's got to be Arthur Godfrey's show!* His cast and crew were rehearsing before going on the air at eight o'clock. *What I'd give to be in there.*

As I turned away, a station wagon pulled up to the curb, and a woman jumped out. She opened the back door, pulled out a cake on a platter and held it with both hands as she stepped up on the sidewalk.

"Would you like me to open the gate for you?" I asked.

"Oh, would you, pleeeze?" she said.

I quickly lifted the latch and folded it back.

"And could you bring in that carton on the backseat for me?"

"You bet!"

I scooped up the carton, slammed the car door and joined her at the gate. She entered the door with me beside her, and we marched into the bright lights of the CBS Theater.

Walking across the stage, we crossed in front of two cameras fixed on pedestals. Men had their faces hidden in the view finders. In the middle aisle, a man sat behind a camera perched on a crane and waited to be lifted in the air. Another stood on a platform above rubber tires and extended a microphone boom over a male quartet. *Just like I pictured only I'm seeing it all for real.* I heard a voice on a speaker giving directions from somewhere in the theater and shivered. It was the voice of Arthur Godfrey.

Gawking at the activity, I avoided bumping into the woman with the cake when she stopped in the far wings. She spoke to me in one breath.

"I'm from the ad agency and had to get the client's props here for tonight's show, but was running late, got held up in traffic and thank you sooo much for your help."

I put the carton down and she pulled out boxes of Pillsbury Cake Mix and arranged them on a table. *She must think I'm someone with CBS. I better leave before she asks me to do something else.* I backed away and melted in with people milling around on the stage.

There they were, the singers I watched on Godfrey's show. Frank Parker, short but dapper in a dark suit, and

Marian Marlowe, thin and wearing heavy eye makeup and a slinky gown. Both looked older in person, but stunning. The three fresh-faced McGuire Sisters clustered together, all smiley under big hairdos. And sitting on a folding chair reading a newspaper was debonair, deep-voiced announcer, Tony Marvin. I was thrilled to be seeing them in person and in color, too.

Godfrey's voice ordered the McGuire's to stand under the boom mike and rehearse their song. The band leader in the orchestra pit raised his baton. *Hey, that's Archie Bleyer!*

The sisters finished their song, and I heard Godfrey again.

"Stay theah. I'm coming down."

I stood offstage and looked at a young man next to me. He nodded.

"Are you in the show?" I asked.

"Yes. I'm singing."

"Oh, are you in a group?"

"No. I'm Pat Boone."

What a dope I was. In the dim light of the wings, I didn't recognize the up-and-coming singer. I recovered from my goof and shook his hand.

"I'm going to a disc jockey school," I gushed. "When I get into radio, maybe I can interview you."

"That would be nice," he said politely.

A stocky man with rusty hair rushed past me, so close we almost touched. I only saw the back of his head as he limped on the stage, but I knew who he was in a heart beat. *That's the man my mother listened to on the radio – who I see emceeing Talent Scouts and hosting this show with his friends.* He sat on a wooden stool and placed a ukulele on his knee. With the McGuire Sisters gathered around, Arthur Godfrey began to rehearse a song. He screwed up the fingering on his uke and stopped playing.

"Oh, shit," he said.

The McGuire's turned away and giggled.

I glanced at my watch. Even though I wanted to stay with those fascinating people in that marvelous setting, I had to leave. Class was about to begin in the building next door.

ONE NIGHT IN CLIFTON

When class ended one night, the school's director stopped me at the door before my run to the bus terminal.
"Would you like to visit WPAT the next time I'm on?" Fred Darwin asked.
"Sure!" I answered.
We arranged to meet the following Sunday during his evening shift.

* * *

I read in *B-T* magazine that Dickens Wright had expanded the music of *Gaslight Review* throughout WPAT's entire broadcast day. Whenever I tuned in, a Broadway show tune, movie theme or love song was playing. The orchestras of Mantovanni, Kostelanetz, Morton Gould and Percy Faith were the featured performers. I never heard a vocalist on the station.
Recordings of "easy listening" music were scarce in 1956, so Wright created ways to stretch the limited library at WPAT. For four hours each afternoon, the station played the identical music, selection by selection, that was aired later on

the evening *Gaslight* program. He called the afternoon offering *Gaslight Previews*.

To pad the schedule, he'd program the same tune back-to-back in a twelve-minute segment, but performed in different styles. It would start with a lush orchestra followed by a jazz combo, a single piano, then finish with another orchestra.

I thought Dickens Wright was a genius.

His unique idea of twelve-minute blocks of uninterrupted music with no chatter from announcers during the breaks in between attracted a large audience in the New York area. WPAT had to open a sales office in Manhattan to handle the increased demand from advertisers. Soon, stations in other markets picked up the success of WPAT and adopted the same format while recording companies began to produce and distribute more easy listening albums. The supply was expanded by Arthur Fiedler's Boston Pops and the orchestra of Robert Farnon became available from England. Even TV's Jackie Gleason wielded a baton in a studio to record an album of sultry ballads featuring the sweet trumpet of Bobbie Hackett. Wright's station was a soothing alternative to the raucous rock and roll sprouting up at other spots on the dial. Dad and Marge kept WPAT on at home all the time.

* * *

The following Sunday, I parked my father's Hudson by the four towers on Broad Street in Clifton, New Jersey. WPAT had moved its operation from downtown Paterson to the transmitter site, and I sat for a moment and watched the red lights on the towers blink on and off in the dusk.

As I approached a windowless cinder block building, I remembered visiting the old location on Hamilton Street. *How exciting the red and gold letters looked on the front glass.* No wording showed on the bunker-like structure in Clifton.

I didn't balk at the door like I did as a kid and didn't need my high school friend to push the button the way I had when I was a teenager. Without hesitation, I rang the bell.

Fred Darwin opened the door. He was dressed in a golf shirt and slacks, different from the suit and tie he wore at the broadcasting school. He led me to a large, uncluttered room, the one and only studio for WPAT.

Bright fluorescent ceiling lights lit walls covered by perforated, pale-yellow tiles. A small control board of knobs and switches sat on a Formica-top table in the middle of the room and a microphone on a boom hung above it. The place smelled like fresh paint.

I looked through a slanted window into the next room. An engineer sat behind the glass, a ponderous black transmitter looming in back of him. *I wonder if the heavy gent I saw at the old place still works for the station.*

"The announcers are allowed to handle all the equipment in the building with one exception," Darwin said. "The engineers in that transmitter room have control of the most important switch, the one that turns our microphone on and off."

We sat at the table, Darwin in a chair on wheels, me on a metal folding one. No turntables were in sight, but four gray cabinets on small rollers surrounded us. Darwin saw my puzzled expression.

"They're Ampex machines," he said.

Intrigued, I inspected the slanted front of one of them. A ten-inch metal reel mounted on the left was filled to the edge with thin brown tape that went under a pick-up head to an empty take-up reel on the right. *Looks like a bigger version of Halsey's table-top Wolensak.*

"Our entire library of vinyl albums has been recorded on reels of tape," Darwin went on. "That eliminates the pops and clicks that develop from too much wear on discs." *I got it. There's no need for turntables and pick-up arms with damaging needles that were used in the old control room on Hamilton Street.*

Music ended on an Ampex. Darwin rolled his chair to the desk and asked for the air from the engineer by pointing at the microphone. *Just like Jazzbo did at WNEW.* I was at Darwin's side when a red bulb came on below the window of the transmitter room. He told listeners what program they were hearing and on what station. A shiver ran over my shoulders. *He's being heard by thousands, maybe millions of people.* The bulb went off, and the engineer began playing a recorded commercial for Northwest Orient Airways.

"Why didn't you announce the tunes?" I asked Darwin.

He handed me a thin stapled booklet with a colorful cover. Inside, titles and orchestras were listed for every selection played in every hour of every day for the entire month. The tiny words made me recall squinting at names jammed in the grids of the old *Radio Guide* in the Sunday paper. I scanned the listing of orchestras and saw names – Mantovanni, Kostelanetz, Morton Gould, Percy Faith.

"A new program guide is sent to listeners on a mailing list every thirty days, so there's not much for us to say," Darwin said.

After a reel had finished on one of the Ampex machines, he rewound it, removed it, put it in a slim white cardboard box and placed it with others on a row of shelves along a wall. He threaded a new reel and sat down. *Pretty neat.*

"To keep the format successful, a strict set of rules must be followed. There are more 'don't's' than 'do's.' One rule forbids the announcers from giving our names on the air, but I'm working on management to convince them otherwise. I feel if we tell the listeners who we are, it'll give a warmer, more personal feeling to the station."

Darwin announced a break at half past the hour and another at quarter to. Reels of the Ampex machines continued to turn, sending music to the four towers outside and into the night sky. I sat, fascinated.

During the fifteen minutes remaining in the hour, I followed Darwin to a waist-high box at the door. He raised the lid, and I heard the familiar chunka-chunka of a teletype. Tearing off a long sheet of paper tumbling in back of the machine, he closed the lid and sound ended. Darwin dragged the paper with me behind careful not to step on it. Seated at the table, I leaned on my elbows and watched his next moves.

Scrolling through the paper, he laid it down and used a ruler to rip out five short news stories clustered in a summary. I thought of the one I had read for him at BCA about the "police" and the "drug store."

Darwin found a weather forecast, ripped it out and checked off three temperatures in the tri-state area. *Man, I'm getting more of an education here than at the school – and for free, too.*

An orchestra filled with strings ended a lush arrangement of a ballad. Darwin sat up, cleared his throat and pointed at the microphone. The red bulb came on again.

"Here's the latest news from the WPAT newsroom." Concentrating on his voice, I didn't realize the "newsroom" was only a teletype machine in a box. He delivered the news without mispronouncing a word or fluffing a line. I was afraid to breathe. When he finished with the weather, the bulb went off, and he pushed a button on the control board.

Reels on an Ampex started to turn and another twelve-minute segment of uninterrupted easy listening music began. *How smooth. How professional.*

When the hour ended, I didn't want to wear out my welcome. I thanked Darwin, shook his hand and told him I'd see him in class on Tuesday. I waved goodbye to the engineer in the transmitter room and left the station.

Driving home, I turned over in my mind what I had seen. *Why did the engineer have control of the microphone instead of Darwin? A union demand maybe? How strange the all the words on the teletype paper were in capital letters. Can I play music from reels of tape and still be a "disc" jockey?*

The director of the broadcasting school had been a savior to me when he corrected my sloppy diction, and watching him at a functioning radio station was a great influence. My Sunday night visit with Fred Darwin in Clifton was an experience I would cherish always.

GETTING THE GIG

I stood outside a building in Manhattan where many of my favorite programs originated besides the ones that were done at Radio City a few blocks away. Arthur Godfrey did his daily show in the morning from a studio that was below-street level, and on floors above, actors and actresses performed soap operas one after another in the afternoon. Before the variety shows and mysteries started in the evening, Edward R. Murrow reported on the world from his renowned newsroom. The radio network was famous for its address in a canyon of advertising agencies. At the door of 485 Madison Avenue, I was about to enter the Columbia Broadcasting System.

* * *

At twelve weeks into the course at the DJ school, Ernie Althschuler sidled up to me one evening. He didn't want the other students to hear, so he motioned for me to follow him into the hall.

"You're ready to go out," he said. "One of my duties at CBS is engineer for *The Galen Drake Show*. The announcer for the program owns three stations in South Carolina. He likes to hire guys out of broadcast schools here because he thinks their Yankee accents lend sophistication to his stations in the swamp grass." Althschuler paused and smiled. "Anyway, I want you to meet Olin Tice."

* * *

I straightened my tie and made sure the new white shirt I bought for the occasion was tucked in. Pushing open the glass door at the blue-tiled entrance, I walked into the lobby for CBS. Trying to sound business-like, I lowered my voice and spoke to the receptionist seated behind a circular counter.

"I'm Dave Archard and I have an appointment with Olin Tice."

She pointed down the hall.

"Press the button for 'Master Control' in any of the elevators."

It was early evening and I was alone as I whooshed up in one of them. *I wonder how many stars I've listened to have ridden in here?*

Olin Tice stood at the door of an announce booth. He looked just like I had pictured network announcers when I was a kid. He was tall and slim in a dark, tailored suit, had black hair, a square jaw and flashing teeth. Back in the forties, when I was eating my breakfast before school, my mother listened to Tice give local news on the network's New York station.

He ushered me into the booth big enough for a desk, boom mike and two chairs.

An engineer sat behind a slanted window with a rack of equipment behind him. From a wall speaker, Bing Crosby and Rosemary Clooney bantered back and forth on their fifteen-minute program from Hollywood. Tice wasted no time.

"My father and I own stations in Lake City, Moncks Corner and Myrtle Beach in South Carolina. My brother-in-law, John Kenworthy, is the manager at WMYB in Myrtle Beach. He needs someone to pull double duty, first to do the morning show from six to nine, then to handle traffic the rest of the day."

Before continuing, Tice held up his hand and rolled his chair to the microphone. The Crosby-Clooney program ended, an announcer in Hollywood said "This is CBS, The Stars' Address" and the engineer pointed to Tice. In a perfectly pitched voice, he said simply: "WCBS, AM and FM, New York." *Whew! He was just heard from Connecticut to the Jersey shore and I'm in the same room with him!* The engineer raised both arms to indicate he had turned off the microphone, *The Jack Smith Show* started on the speaker, and Olin Tice was able to talk again.

"I'm going to Myrtle Beach in a week. Can you get an audition of yourself on a disc to take with me?"

"Yes, I can," I answered confidently.

We arranged to meet again, and I floated out to the elevators. Dropping to the lobby, I wondered why Tice made the strange request for my audition to be on a *disc* instead of a reel of tape. *How am I going to get that done?*

As the train swayed toward home, my mind flashed on a word Tice had used when explaining the job in Myrtle Beach. Bill Maher at BCA confirmed the definition given in my hard-cover radio book for the word "traffic" – only he put it in stronger terms.

"Working with orders from the sales department, a traffic person prepares the station's schedule or 'log' for each day of the week. It shows an hour per page with advertisers' commercials or 'spots' typed in red. As an announcer, you must get those messages on the air, or you'll bring the wrath of the sales manager down on you." It sounded like a snap job to me. Of course I hadn't told Olin

Tice I planned to be a disc jockey and move up to the big time as soon as possible.

* * *

While walking on Broadway to the DJ school, I spotted a sign at a door in Times Square: "Recording Studio One Flight Up." *I wonder if...*

The following evening with no class, I jumped on a bus after work and rode down to the door in Times Square. I ventured up the flight of stairs and was met at the top by a young man not much older than me. He shook my hand, said his name was Ben, and that he was the owner, producer and engineer for the recording studio.

"Can I get an audition of myself on a disc?" I asked.

"Sure. Come in."

Sitting at a beat-up table in his cramped quarters, Ben asked my name. He switched on a gooseneck lamp, and in the dim light we cobbled together a short presentation of my limited talent.

The man must have produced announcer auditions before. He yanked open the bent drawer of a metal file cabinet and pulled out a coffee-stained piece of commercial copy. I took crumpled headlines from my pocket that I had fished out of a trash can in the ABC newsroom. With the stub of a pencil, I scribbled a record intro on the margin, then faced Ben's dented microphone.

"Let's try doing it," he said.

Each time I stumbled over a word, I stopped and gritted my teeth, embarrassed at my lack of professionalism.

"That's okay. Keep going," Ben said over his control board. "The tape's rolling."

On the fourth take with no fluffs, he called out.

"That's the one!"

I stepped around to where he sat and saw I'd been recorded on an Ampex machine like the ones at WPAT. To satisfy the strange request by Olin Tice, Ben transferred the audition on the tape to a disc.

After placing a sharp needle down to a black platter spinning on a turntable, he pushed a button on the Ampex, and my voice cut into grooves of the acetate surface. *Gee, I sound clearer than on Halsey's Wolensak.* With a small artist's brush, Ben kept sweeping a curly thread that built around the needle until my three-minute bit ended. He wiped the disc clean and asked my name again.

"It's Dave Archer, right?"

I corrected him, and he printed "Audition: Dave Archard" on the label with a marking pen and slipped the disc in a green paper jacket. I paid him, thanked him and went down the stairs clutching my first chance for landing a job in radio.

* * *

Back at CBS, I was met by Olin Tice outside master control. I handed him the disc with a crisp copy of my "rez-a-may" tucked neatly in the jacket. We arranged to meet when he returned from South Carolina.

The days dragged, but the job at ABC and classes at the school kept me busy. I thought about what I had done on the disc. *I hope the brother-in-law in Myrtle Beach likes it.* Finally, the evening came to enter 485 Madison Avenue one more time. As he did twice before, Tice got right to the point.

"John Kenworthy liked your audition."

My heart jumped. *Somebody recognizes my ability!* It was either that, or there was no other guy coming out of a broadcasting school soon, and the brother-in-law in South Carolina was desperate.

"You'll replace a girl doing traffic at WMYB," Tice continued. "She's agreed to stay on to train you before she starts college. The need for an announcer is imminent. You'll get two paychecks each week, one for thirty five dollars with deductions taken out for the traffic job, and a flat fifteen dollar talent fee for doing the morning show." *Gee, I'm going to be paid for being a "talent."*

"How soon can you leave for Myrtle Beach?" he asked.

"Right away," I blurted. Of course I had to give notice to Joe at ABC and tell Fred Darwin at BCA I was leaving, but we set a date and sealed the deal with a handshake. As I walked to the elevators, Olin Tice called after me.

"Keep your nose clean, kid."

I knew what the term meant, but wondered how it related to a job in radio. Boy, did I have a lot to learn.

HEADING OUT TO RADIOLAND

My finger went down through pink Delaware, green Maryland and yellow Virginia on the colorful map of the United States spread on my bed. Under tan North Carolina, I found light blue South Carolina. *Now, where's Myrtle Beach?*

The town had "beach" in its name, so my finger traced the coast. It didn't go far. Just below the shared border of the Carolinas and right on the Atlantic, it stopped at the small town with the small station for my first job in radio. *Okay, how do I get there?*

Driving the Plymouth wasn't an option. I had sold the car to a junk yard for $20 when I started riding the Susquehanna. The old car wouldn't have gotten me past New Brunswick in Jersey anyway. I had to find a city close to Myrtle Beach with a bus station, a boat dock, a runway – anything.

My finger moved two inches inland to Florence. Roads spread out in all directions, and a line with barbs indicating a railroad ran through it. *That's it! I'll hop a train at Penn Station in Newark and ride the rails to Florence, South Carolina. To get over to Myrtle Beach, I'll do what people do in New York. Take a cab.*

* * *

If the American Broadcasting Company was crushed when I gave notice to Joe, I'm sure I was replaced right away with another young budding radio personality eager to operate a mimeograph machine. Charlie Heinz told me he was accepted into ABC's producer training program and would start by timing news stories in the radio division.

At the end of my last class at Broadcast Coaching Associates, I said good bye to my fellow students. Sal with the withered arm inspected the fingernails on his good hand.

"See ya," he said.

Pearl looked up from her knitting.

"God bless you, son," she said.

Busty Tammy surprised me with a hug.

I was too wrapped up with my good fortune to ask what they were going to do when they finished the course. Sal had promise. He had a deep voice and talked about Elvis a lot.

* * *

The Saturday evening before I left for Myrtle Beach, Jerry Van Riper invited me to his folks' rambling house in Upper Ridgewood. I walked out on their lighted patio and was shocked to see my friends home from college for the summer. When they saw me, they lifted bottles of Coca Cola and shouted.

"Surprise!"

There were ex-jocks from the football team, former cheerleaders, even reporters I worked with on *High Times*. Dailey, Hayes, Hopper, Norton, Wells and Halsey Sheffield were there, too. Mr. and Mrs. Van Riper stood off to the side, smiling.

The gang pulled me over to a giant cardboard box painted like a cake, and Bill Dailey yelled. "We have a present for you, Arch."

Joan Verdon, wearing short shorts and a tight t-shirt, popped up through the top. She threw her arms in the air and laughed. Joan was one of the girls I could relax around and kid with when in high school. Taking her hand, I helped her out of the box. I was tickled she was at the party.

As we sipped soda and scooped potato chips into onion dip, a few of the guys told me they weren't going back to college in the fall, but were joining the Army. Van Riper said he was going in the Marines. I wondered if any of my friends envied me for starting my chosen profession so early in life, or if they thought I was making a big mistake.

Sunday, I sealed my high school yearbook and *Radio, the Fifth Estate* in a box and stored it in the basement of Dad's house. Packing was easy. Clothes and the framed third-class license fit nicely in the suitcase Dad let me borrow.

I had asked Halsey at the party the night before if he'd drive me to Penn Station in Newark. As soon as he pulled up to the house in his family's station wagon, I walked over to my father seated with the Sunday paper on his lap. I stuck out my hand.

"So long, Dad."

Producing oriental figurines for gift shops had not worked out for my father, so he had returned to the business he knew best, automobiles. He was hired to handle the books for an importer in Fort Lee, New Jersey, who brought Volkswagens over from Germany.

Dad was given a Beetle to drive, but it was hard for him to get his long legs into the little car. His fedora was knocked off every time he scrunched behind the wheel.

Dad shook my hand.

"Well, good luck," he said.

In his way, I believe my father was pleased with the venture I was beginning, but didn't say so. I'm sure he was glad I was getting out of his house, so he and Marge could be alone.

Marge came out of the kitchen drying her hands on a towel. I went over and hugged her, and she hugged back. Although Dad didn't tell me then, she would soon become my stepmother.

When Halsey honked, I grabbed the suitcase and flew out the door.

As we drove through the woods of Franklin Lakes, I told my friend about the people I had met since high school and what I did at ABC and the DJ school. He laughed when I described how I followed the agency woman with the cake into the CBS Theater. Filling him in on the job waiting in Myrtle Beach, I left out the part about doing the traffic thing. I wanted him to think I was starting as a true on-air personality.

When we came into Upper Ridgewood, I glanced at the big houses with the wide lawns and thought of the fun I'd had with Halsey's tape recorder in his grandmother's mansion on the hill.

At the Erie station downtown, we dove under the railroad that took Frankie Ketz and me to WPAT in Paterson. I remembered how I had balked at the door of the radio station only to go through it later as a teenager with Bob Chambers.

Halsey swung onto Ridgewood Avenue, and I saw Drapkin's store. My mind flashed on finding *White's Radio Log* there, and how I used it at night to bring stations into my radio from cities thousands of miles away.

Rushing past the Warner Theater, I smiled and recalled Saturday matinees in the forties when I joined hundreds of noisy kids to see two, count 'em, two movies.

We cruised by the stately red brick high school. Glimpsing at the football field, I remembered how I ran like Jerry Lewis at the pep rally and did my dying act on the mud of the fifty-yard line.

Up the hill and past the First Presbyterian Church, I pictured the Teen Canteen in the basement and wondered if girls still sat in the dark room on Friday nights and waited for boys to ask them to dance.

I didn't ask Halsey to turn on Kenilworth Avenue and drive by the old stone school or to go down Albert Place and see the neat little house where I lived with Mom, Dad and Tom. I had a train to catch.

As the car bumped along Route 17, I gazed at the giant tower at Lodi for WABC, and Martin Block, Ernie Kovacs and Charlie Heinz came to mind. I could almost smell the machines in the messy mimeograph room.

As we sped past Teterboro Airport, the waving reeds of the Jersey swamps made me relive the thrill of riding through there in Dad's car at night and seeing radio towers wink their lights at me.

Looking at the skyline of Manhattan, I recalled the day I visited Channel 9 in the Empire State Building with Johnny Clark, the afternoon I sat next to Jazzbo while he did his show on WNEW and the morning I lacked the nerve to go in the studio at WINS to meet Bob and Ray.

Halsey barely stopped the station wagon at the curb of Penn Station when I shook his hand, grabbed my suitcase and jumped out.

"See y' later, Halls," I called over my shoulder as I ran into the terminal.

* * *

The train pulled out into the sunlight, the increasing hum of the diesel engine interrupted from time to time by a blaring horn. How different from the chugging locomotives and wailing whistles I heard as a kid in bed at night. Through a smeared window, I watched the scenery change from truck stops and oil refineries to the green fields of the New Jersey I knew. Tucking my suitcase beside me, I settled back in my seat. *I'm the luckiest guy in the world. I'm finally going to live my dream.*

As I've grown older, I've realized there's no such thing as luck. Good things happen to people who struggle and work hard to achieve a goal – when preparation meets opportunity. Looking back, my preparation began as early as age nine when characters streamed into my bedroom radio and ignited a passion in me to fly on the airwaves, too. As a young man, I was presented the opportunity when the instructor at the DJ school had me meet the station owner at CBS.

My ticket showed stops in Philadelphia, Baltimore and one at night in Richmond.

A porter wearing a white apron started down the aisle selling sandwiches and soda from a tray hanging from his neck. The swaying of the car and rhythmic clickity-clack of the wheels would help me sleep sitting up as the train went deeper into Dixie.

It was June 1956. I was twenty years old and finally on my way to being a radio announcer. I was excited and a little scared.

HELLO FLORENCE AND MYRTLE

A conductor banged open the door of the Pullman car. "Florence, next stop! Florence!"

As the train approached the city in South Carolina, I worried of what lay ahead.

Playing radio at the DJ school was fun, but can I handle a job in an actual control room? What if I mess up? Will I be treated as a wet-nosed beginner? I looked outside at a field of cows then reached for my suitcase as the train slowed down.

Humid air hit me when I stepped on the platform of the railroad station. Carrying the suitcase, I walked along the warped boards. In the faded mirror of a gum machine, I saw wisps of hair sticking out from my head from the train trip. A comb and brush were packed in the suitcase, so I smoothed my hair as best I could with my hand. Tucking in my white shirt to wrinkled chinos, I figured I'd be cooler if I rolled up the sleeves. *I hope people at the radio station won't think I'm a bum when I arrive at the door.*

Two drinking fountains were in an alcove of the train station, one labeled "White Only," the other "Colored." I knew what segregation was, but was confronted with it for the first time. I realized there were racial barriers back home, too, but seeing the fountains gave me an uncomfortable feeling. I was in someplace far different than New Jersey.

I put the suitcase down to collect my thoughts. *Okay, I've come this far. Now, how am I going to get to Myrtle Beach?*

A mud-splattered car was parked at the end of the platform. The black four-door sedan reminded me of my beat-up Plymouth except for the faded letters on the side, "Taxi." I approached the driver slumped behind the steering wheel reading a newspaper.

"Can you drive me over to Myrtle Beach?" I asked.

The man put down the paper and took the stub of a cigar out of his mouth.

"Cost y'all twenty bucks," he said.

With money left from training at the broadcasting school, I was flush with cash. Opening the back door, I threw the suitcase on the seat and climbed in.

"Okay," I said.

The taxi roared alive, bounced over the railroad tracks and skidded onto a two-lane road of pot holes. I rolled down the window to let air rush in. Gazing at rows of red dirt in the flat farm land of South Carolina, my mind wandered back to the trees and grass of suburban New Jersey. Round signs on the side of the road flashed by every few miles, with the words "Dr. Pepper 10, 2, 4." *What the heck is that?* I sat back in the dusty seat, and the bumping of the taxi made me nod off to sleep.

When the taxi turned onto a smoother four-lane highway, the driver called back over his shoulder. "We're in Myrtle Beach, son. Where do you wanna be left off?"

I shook my head to clear it.

"The radio station."

"I know the town," he said. "I know where it is."

The taxi roared again. After two blocks, it turned onto an unpaved street. Spotting a thin steel tower ahead, I sat on the edge of the seat, and my heart beat faster. In a grove of palm trees was a white cinder-block building. It looked like a private home, but as the taxi drew closer, I saw black letters above the door: W M Y B. I almost cheered.

Before the taxi stopped, I opened the door and waved a twenty dollar bill at the driver. He reached around and plucked it from my hand as I grabbed the suitcase and jumped out. The taxi spun around, spit sand from its wheels and sped back to the highway.

I stood for a moment. *This is it. This is what I've wanted since I was a kid.* I thought of the tour at NBC and the visit to WPAT, looking through slanted windows and wishing so much to be part of the action. The small building in front of me wasn't Radio City or even the station in Paterson, but it was a place with a microphone, turntables and a chance to be on the air. I picked up the suitcase and stepped on the gravel path leading to the door and my destiny.

MEET AND GREET

A man with freckles and orange-framed glasses walked across the red linoleum floor of the lobby and stuck out his hand.

"Dave Archard! I'm John Kenworthy. Boy, have we been waiting for you." The manager of WMYB pulled me toward him.

"Glad to be here," I said, trying to keep my balance.

Dressed in tan slacks and a shirt ablaze with tropical flowers, the brother-in-law looked different from Olin Tice in New York with his tailored suit and narrow tie.

Kenworthy took me by the arm.

"Donna, this is Dave." A girl about my age with dark eyes and long black hair looked up from a typewriter.

"He's going to take your place doing the log when you return to school."

She smiled at me and I smiled back.

I glanced around the lobby at three desks, wicker chair and an end table strewn with magazines. Soda and snack dispensers stood together with a water cooler on one side and a teletype machine on the other.

"Phil, come meet Dave," Kenworthy said. A man with white hair grunted as he got up from a desk.

"Mr. Rice here is our top salesman, and he does the news at noon." The man didn't smile, but gripped my hand.

Kenworthy motioned with his hand.

"C'mon, let's see Jerry."

He hurried to a door as the light of a red On Air sign went off beside it. Before the manager turned the handle, the door swung open, and a short young man appeared. "Jerry Girard, here's Dave Archard," Kenworthy said. We shook hands. "Jerry's our jack-of-all-trades announcer around here." Girard looked at me and shrugged.

"Hamp Smith, our other salesman, will be here soon," Kenworthy went on, "but you probably want to get settled in your room." *Thank goodness. My brain is swirling with all these names and faces.*

"I've made arrangements for you at a boarding house. It's right across Ocean Highway. Ask for Mrs. McGarrity, the landlady."

He whisked me to the front door. Before I knew it, I was outside on the gravel path. Walking with the suitcase to the highway, I turned and looked back at the simple building with four letters above the door. *I can't wait to get back in there.*

* * *

The boarding house was halfway up a sand dune on a road of crushed shells. It was covered with clapboard siding bleached gray by the sun. A porch with screens bulging from wind off the ocean wrapped around the front and sides. A small stooped-over woman stood on the steps watering pots of flowers.

"You must be David," she said. "I'm Mrs. McGarrity. Let me show you your room." I followed her inside, and we climbed a worn staircase to the second floor. Either her bones creaked or the wood did under our feet.

"Mr. Kenworthy said you're from New York City," she said as we walked along a hall filled with cooking odors.

"Outside in New Jersey, actually," I said.

We stopped at a door, and she turned the white porcelain knob.

"Here's your room."

A floral print spread covered the single bed sticking out from one wall. A pine wood chest of drawers stained dark brown stood opposite. A tangle of wire hangers hung in a closet with no door, and lace curtains blew into the room at the one open window. I caught sight of white sand sloping down to the frothy surf of the Atlantic.

"You and Jerry will share the bathroom between your room and his. He works at the radio station, too."

"Yeah, I know. I just met him."

"I change the sheets and towels once a week." She put her hand on my arm. "No drinking and no women. If you must smoke, walk up to the beach."

Booze, sex and cigarettes. What's the chance of that? Just one time in high school, my buddies and I bought a six-pack of Rheingold at a road house across the state line in Suffern. I had agonized at the phone before asking Roberta Bayer to the senior prom. And smoking! A few puffs of an Old Gold made my fingers turn cold and my stomach queasy. Still, with my twenty-first birthday months away, the landlady's rules made me feel very adult.

"The room costs twenty dollars a week," she said, "paid in advance." I pulled a twenty from my wallet and gave it to her. "That includes supper every night. We all eat together promptly at six." *Hey, chow's part of the deal.*

The land lady left the room, pulling the door closed behind her. I looked around at the new quarters. It was different from my bedroom in Dad's house with the chubby radio on the nightstand and the clunky TV at the foot of the bed. I realized again I was away from home and on my own.

The long day of train, taxi and greetings caught up to me. Exhausted, I flopped on the bed and sank into the musty-smelling spread. *I'll be down for dinner at six, Mrs. McGarrity.*

LEARNING THE ROPES

The lure of the ocean was too much the next morning. I pulled on swim trunks from the suitcase and ran to the beach.

I plunged into the surf and broke the wave behind it. Swimming out, I thrashed the water until my arms tired from the vigorous strokes. The warm blue-green Atlantic washed away the whirlwind activity of the day before.

My legs fought the tug of the outgoing tide as I waded to shore. Placing one of Mrs. McGarrity's towels on the soft white sand, I stretched out to soak up the sun on the Grand Strand of coastal Carolina. A shout interrupted the serenity.

"Hey, Dave!"

Turning over, I looked up. Jerry Girard stood at the top of the dune waving his arms. He shouted again.

"C'mere!"

I got up, grabbed the towel and stumbled across the soft sand to reach him.

"Kenworthy's mad as hell," he said. "He wants you in the station right away." *Of course! My job! The reason for being here. What the hell was I thinking?*

Rushing to my room, I threw on the only clothes handy, the same ones I wore the day before on the train. *I should have hung everything from the suitcase instead of going to the beach.* Brushing sand from my feet, I shoved them into loafers without putting on socks.

It was tricky running down the shell road and buttoning my shirt at the same time.

Between traffic on Ocean Highway, I dashed across, my loafers barely touching the asphalt. *Am I gonna be labeled a screw-up on my first day?* I skidded to a stop at the station and smoothed my hair.

John Kenworthy stood at the door, his smiley face changed to a scowl.

"I don't need you lying on the beach. I need you here. Jerry and Carl have been pulling double duty, and they're tired. Get in the control room and learn the equipment. You're going on the air tonight."

With head down, I felt like a kid being sent to bed without dinner. *Wait a minute. Did he say I was going on the air tonight?* Straightening up like a bolt of lightning hit me, I hurried to the room with the microphone and turntables.

A young man with brown curly hair sat at a u-shaped desk. He finished setting up a record on a turntable.

"You're Dave, right?" He rose, extended his six-foot-two frame and put out his hand. "I'm Carl Grand."

He pointed at the station's control board.

"Well, here it is."

A gray monster lay across the desk. Bumps of knobs, switches and buttons on the front looked intimidating. As if in greeting, I touched its metal skin and felt warmth from its innards. The sweet aroma coming up was exciting in spite of my growing anxiety. *Will this thing be my friend?*

Green knobs ran across the bottom of the control board. Althschuler at the broadcasting school called them "pots." Switches with rubber tips stood above each, some straight, others leaning to the right. Along the top, a few black buttons were pushed in, others remaining out.

"Okay, here's how you handle this baby," Carl said.

He sat in a chair on wheels, pulled himself up to the control board and ran his fingers across the pots.

"This one's for the control room microphone, then the mike in the studio, the three turntables, network, church remote on Sunday and the reel-to-reel tape machine." *Whoa, slow down.* With no labels to identify the pots, I tried to memorize each one as quickly as Carl named them. He tapped the last one on the right.

"Don't touch this one. It feeds the board to the transmitter and stays where it is. Forget the buttons up top. Just leave 'em alone."

"Don't touch."

"Leave alone."

My brain was beginning to fry.

In the middle of the control board, a needle danced to music behind the glass front of a meter. The music ended and the needle fell to the left only to bounce up when applause started.

"How come I hear music, but nothing's spinning on the turntables?" I said.

"That's Bert Parks' *Bandstand* coming out of New York on NBC," Carl replied. "The owner up North thinks the network lends class to his station here." He rolled his eyes to the ceiling. I saw no network affiliation for WMYB when I looked up the station in *White's Radio Log*, so NBC was a surprise.

Turntables and pick-up arms were built into both wings of the desk. A larger turntable and a long straight pick-up arm sat in a gray cabinet on wheels, the letters R C A in an oval on the side. I ran my fingers over the ridges of the rubber pad on the turntable.

"You ever see one of those?" Carl said.

"I sure have," I said in a whisper as my fingers ran over the ridges of the rubber pad on the turntable. I recalled admiring the big turntables at ABC until the dinky one with curved arm at the DJ school came to mind. *This one's for professionals.*

A microphone hung over the control board from a boom. A black wire coiled its way along the boom, wrapped around the stand and disappeared under the desk like a snake. *That's like the one I saw at Radio City.*

A large clock encased in a sculpted wooden frame was fastened to the wall. A thin red hand stuttered around the Roman numerals on the face. *It's exactly like the one at WPAT.*

"Use that clock to join programs on the nose from NBC," Carl continued. "I check its accuracy every morning with a special radio in back of the transmitter that tells the exact time." *Maybe I should be taking notes. I'm getting a headache.*

To the left of the desk was a slanted window. With a sweep of my eye, I took inventory of everything in the studio on the other side. A chair was pulled up to a table with a desk mike in the middle. In one corner, a plant with wilted leaves in need of water stood next to a black piano, its yawning top held open by a stick.

"That's where Mr. Rice does the news," Carl said. He leaned back in the chair and put his elbows on the padded arms.

"You shoulda been here last week," he said. "I didn't know the red bulb in there had burnt out. When it was time for him to begin the news, I turned on his mike. There's no need to throw Rice a cue because he always starts when the bulb comes on. So there he was with his mike wide open, waiting for the light to go on. Before I could point to him, he said 'I'll be a witch's tit. When're ya going to turn on my mike?' That went out on the air from the North Carolina border to Georgetown south of here." I laughed, but my headache was growing worse.

The transmitter, a hulking box of gray steel, squatted in the back of the control room and hummed quietly. I walked over and peeked through the square glass window on the front. Cucumber-shaped glass tubes stood in a row and glowed yellow. The transmitter was sending *Bandstand* on a thick black cable through the wall to the tower in back of the station. *My voice'll be going out from that tower in a few short hours.* My stomach flipped.

I lifted a clipboard off a nail on the wall.

"That's the transmitter log," Carl said. "Remember, the FCC wants us to take meter readings every half-hour. If you miss one, just make up the numbers."

He got out of the chair and went behind the transmitter.

"Look here," he said and I followed. "This is the radio for the Naval Observatory in Colorado. Click the left-hand knob, and a voice will tell you the time to the second." *I'll listen to it later. I want to hear the voice from Colorado.*

Carl pointed to a cork board covered with yellowed memos, faded newspaper clippings and cartoons.

"Find room on there and pin up your license."

He waved pages of paper stapled together.

"Here's the program log Donna types. She's a looker isn't she? But be careful. Her boyfriend plays football at the university in Columbia." *Well, that wipes out any thought of pursuing a future with Donna.*

I opened a narrow door next to the transmitter and looked in at a sink and toilet.

"Oh, yeah," Carl said. "People from the office come in here to use the john. I've told them how many times to wait until the On Air sign goes off in the lobby before barging in."

Just then, Phil Rice entered the control room and hurried into the bathroom. I pretended to inspect boxes of teletype paper stacked against the back wall until I heard the toilet flush. He reappeared, drying his hands with a paper towel.

"Time to do the news," he said and exited.

A moment later, I saw him enter the studio with a fistful of reports ripped from the teletype machine. He sat and scanned the material through rimless glasses perched on his nose.

"I changed the red bulb in there last week," Carl said, "so there's no chance for another outburst from Rice. He's an old retired railroad man. Phil's okay."

When the clock hit noon, Carl Grand's training session ended, and I slumped in a chair. He flipped switches on the monster on the desk and *News at Noon from Coastal Carolina* began. I sat up and tried not to miss a thing.

FIRST TIME

I was left alone in the control room at eight that evening.

Jerry Girard had come in at noon while Mr. Rice was on with the news. I sat behind him and attempted to absorb everything he did all afternoon. I was frazzled when his shift ended at 8 p.m. *Henry J. Taylor and the News* came on from NBC, and Jerry rose from the chair.

"Be sure you lock up when you leave at midnight," he said. "Kenworthy gave you a key, didn't he?"

I said he did and watched Jerry go out the door. The room became quiet except for Mr. Taylor's voice droning from a speaker in the background. My legs were rubbery as I approached the chair waiting for me with open arms.

Sitting on the edge of the seat, I ran my fingers along the pots of the control board and tried to remember which did which. My hands were sweaty, and butterflies fluttered in my stomach. I hadn't felt like leaving the station to grab some food while Jerry was on, and the soda and snacks of the vending machines in the lobby had no appeal. Finally, my brain yelled, "Get started!"

I picked up the program log and read that Mr. Taylor ended his news at 8:14:30. *Okay, that's fourteen minutes and thirty seconds past eight.* I looked at the clock. It was 8:07.

The letters "PSA" and "ID" showed in the break between Mr. Taylor and the program that followed from NBC at 8:15. *Settle down, settle down.* I remembered what I learned at the broadcast school. A "PSA" was a Public Service Announcement and an "ID" was station identification with call letters and city-of-license. *Let's see, with thirty seconds to fill between programs that's twenty for a "PSA" and ten for an "ID." Now, what do I read?*

I had watched Jerry deliver commercials and messages from a copy book on a metal stand on top of the control board. Right there, staring me in the face was a PSA for U.S. Savings Bonds. My mind raced. *Okay, okay, now the "ID."*

Station slogans scrawled on cards were taped to the wall. I selected one and rehearsed the two elements for my debut. Glancing first at the red second hand on the clock, I read the Savings Bond PSA out loud. My eyes darted to the card and I delivered a slogan with call letters. I looked back at the clock. The hand had moved 29 seconds. *Perfect!*

The time was 8:11. My mouth was dry, and I wished I had brought a wax cup of water into the control room. *Do I dare run out to the water cooler in the lobby? What if Mr. Taylor ends his program early, or the door slams and locks in back of me, or I slip and fall and hit my head?* I stayed in the security of the chair, its arms wrapped around me.

Henry J. Taylor wrapped up his news. I had no idea what he had been talking about since eight o'clock, but when he said "Good night,' I sat straight in the chair. I looked at the microphone in front of me, the slots of its silver head grinning at me. The announcer in New York closed off Taylor's program.

"This is NBC, the National Broadcasting Company." The chimes rang, "bing, bang, bong." *Oh, God, here goes.* I turned on the microphone.

I delivered the Savings Bond message, hoping my voice wouldn't crack. Still, nervousness made it sound constricted, thin and high. Glancing at the meter on the control board, I saw the words I was speaking bounce the needle behind the glass.

The "ID" followed. I took a quick breath. *Don't rush, but get it in on time.*

"1450 on the dial, this is WMYB, where the Pines meet the Palms in Myrtle Beach, South Carolina." There was a second of silence before the Boston Symphony swept in at 8:15. I turned off the microphone, sat back and smiled. I had become a radio announcer.

Don't stop! What's next? The log showed the Boston Symphony stayed on until nine p.m. then the science fiction drama *X Minus One* followed from NBC. *Good!* Forty-five minutes gave me plenty of time to pick records for the music programs I was to do, popular songs after the *X* program until 10 p.m., dance music until 11, then rhythm and blues until sign-off at midnight.

Getting up from the chair, my legs weren't so rubbery. It was a short walk to three shelves stacked on cinder blocks at both ends. Carl Grand laughingly called the eight-foot pine planks "the music library."

I was attracted first by the bright covers of albums on the top shelf. Shuffling through them, I pulled one out. *Oh, man, 'Ella Fitzgerald Sings the Cole Porter Songbook!'* I leaned that one against the bottom shelf.

The next album featured a singer who was new to me. Flipping over the cover, I read that the young man in the photo was discovered singing in a jazz club while attending college in San Francisco. I had to hear what this Johnny Mathis sounded like, so I put his album down on the floor with the Fitzgerald LP.

Watching the clock, I picked 45 rpm records off the middle shelf. It was easy to find songs by Doris Day, Dean Martin, The Four Lads and other popular singers of the day.

Choosing music for the dance program wasn't difficult. I went back to the top shelf and snatched albums by the big bands of Les Brown and Harry James and even one by Lester Lanin's high society orchestra. I returned to the desk, my arms loaded with music. The phrase "happy as a kid in a candy store" came to my mind. *Tonight, I'm that kid.*

The program log had a break scheduled with a "PSA" and "ID" when the Boston Symphony ended. The next message in the copy book was for The South Carolina Fish and Wildlife Management. I rehearsed it out loud and chose a station slogan on the wall as butterflies continued to flutter in my stomach.

When the announcer in Boston wrapped up the symphony program, I snapped to attention. The network chimes rang and I swallowed hard. *Here we go again.* Delivering the PSA for fish and wildlife, I tried to sound like the announcer who had preceded me on the network. The ID was next.

"This is WMYB, 1450 on your dial, serving Coastal Carolina from Myrtle Beach. The time is nine o'clock." I rejoined NBC, and *X Minus One* began. *Made it, right on the nose!*

The science fiction drama gave me a half-hour to muster a bit more composure. My fingers stopped shaking, but in thirty minutes, the programming would be totally in my hands, sweaty as they were.

I looked ahead at the last pages of the log. Two words jumped out at eleven o'clock: "NEWS - LOC." That meant a "newscast" done "locally" – not by someone at NBC in New York, but by me in Myrtle Beach.

The teletype machine in the lobby! Paper must be running all over the floor. I didn't want to leave the control room, afraid *X Minus One* might go off and leave a dreadful space of dead air. Forcing myself from the chair, I propped open the door with a trash can so it wouldn't slam and lock. I dashed to the lobby. *Oh, don't let me down, NBC.*

Tearing a long sheet from the teletype, I ran back to the control room, the paper flapping behind me. Scrolling through the information, I found a five-minute news summary hot off the wires of the Associated Press, and ripped the pages out with a ruler. I looked at the clock. 9:13. *Okay, plenty of time to read over the news to rehearse any difficult names.*

Hold on! The pop music at 9:30! Where're the records? They were right where I put them at the end of the control board. I fumbled with a little 45 disc, cued it up on a turntable and sat back. Biting my thumb nail, I heard my mother's voice: "Stop it."

I leaned forward and put my head in my hands. *Think, think. Don't let this thing get ahead of you. The music changes from pop songs to dance tunes at ten. No problem there, but Frantic 'Lantic Beach Party follows the news at eleven.* I racked my brain to remember what Jerry told me when he opened the top of my head like Carl and poured in information from a fire hose. *Oh, yeah, I get to play rhythm-and-blues like Alan Freed in New York!* The clock was getting dangerously close to 9:30. *Dare I look for those records now? Go ahead. Do it!*

I jumped from the chair and hurried to "the music library" again. At the end of the shelf with the 45s, I scooped up ones by Bo Diddley, LaVern Baker, Hank Ballard and others. *I hope they're the ones Negro listeners want to hear after the white folks go to bed.*

Back at the control board, *X Minus One* was ending. The log didn't show a name for the program I was about to do, but I was ready with one. I waited until NBC rang the third "bong" of the chimes then turned on the microphone. *Here goes nothing.*

"WMYB presents *Night Music*."

I started a turntable, and Johnnie Ray began singing "Please Mr. Sun." Not realizing the irony of a program of "night" music starting off with a "sun" song, I was thrilled with what just happened. I had become a disc jockey.

It was a joy to open my mike and talk. After playing singer Mel Torme's "Mountain Greenery," I thought I was clever by referring to him as "The Velvet Fog." When Ella Fitzgerald ended "Just One of Those Things," I called her just "Ella," trying to emulate Jazzbo on WNEW. As the new young singer Johnny Mathis sang "Angel Eyes" from his album, I had to stop my activity with the turntables and sit back and listen to him. I went on the air when he finished, said "Wow" and hoped the listeners did, too.

The more I announced, the more relaxed I became. My voice wasn't sounding as pinched as it did when I started at eight o'clock. However, a strange feeling came over me. *I'm alone in a room talking to myself.*

Switching to dance music at ten, I threw in vocals by Jo Stafford and Tony Bennett between the bands of Les Brown and Harry James. The job of selecting records, setting them up and going on the air was no job at all. *I could do this the rest of my life.*

A thought snapped me out of the euphoria. *Oh, my gosh, the news at 11!* I touched the pile of stories at the end of the desk for reassurance. *But what if something big happened in the world since I ripped them off the teletype? Should I go out and check the machine? What if the needle sticks on a record while I'm gone, and the same note plays over and over?*

I took a leap of faith from the chair and flung open the door of the control room, forgetting to prop it with the trash can. Running into the lobby, I slid to a stop at the teletype machine. Tearing off paper, I ran back. The door was wide open and Lester Lanin's ricky-ticky orchestra continued to play without missing a beat. I scrolled through the paper. No earthquake or plane crash had occurred.

There has to be something else. I slapped my forehead. *Weather!* I saw Jerry tape the forecast for Coastal Carolina from the teletype to the wall. I read it through rapidly to myself, barely mumbling the words: "Partlycloudytonight. Low70.SunnyWednesdaywithscatteredafternoonshowers. High88." *Good.*

The hands of the clock were moving up to news time. I put on the last dance number from the Harry James LP, then flipped through the pages of the news stories one more time. *I've got to remember to pronounce the last name of Secretary of State John Foster Dulles as "Dull-us."* When the James band ended, I cleared my throat and became a newsman.

"It's eleven o'clock, and here's the news from the wires of the Associated Press and the WMYB newsroom." It sounded impressive to say "the WMYB newsroom," but it was only a teletype machine in the lobby.

I delivered each item clearly, remembering how Peter Roberts sounded on Bob and Ray's morning show. Ending the news, I gave the weather forecast, adding what was supposed to be the current temperature. I had failed to look out the back window at the thermometer hanging on the sash, so I guessed at it.

"It's...72 degrees under the moon and stars of Myrtle Beach." I hoped it was a clear night. I hadn't thought to check the sky condition by peeking out the front door. *I have to get off my fanny more tomorrow night.*

Reaching over, I started a turntable. Otis Williams and the Charms began singing "Ling, Ting, Tong" and *Frantic 'Lantic Beach Party* hit the air.

The voice of Alan Freed resounded in my head. *Should I sound raw and guttural like him? Nope, just be myself, whoever that is.* I recalled reading how Freed kept his microphone open on WINS and slapped a phone book in time to the music. *Could I do that here in Myrtle Beach? Better not. If I slap this thin desk top, the pick-up arm will jump off the record.*

"Wait a minute. What should I be doing while I'm sitting here?" I said out loud.

"Transmitter readings!"

I hadn't been to the humming hulk in the back of the control room all evening. A Federal Communications Commission law demanded that numbers pointed at by needles in three meters along the front had to be entered on a transmitter log every half hour. I pulled the clipboard off the nail. Lines were empty on the page from eight p.m. on. *What if an FCC inspector walks in right now and sees no readings? I'll be banished from radio forever after being on the air just one night!* I looked at the last entry Jerry wrote, and copied his numbers down to the bottom of the page.

Is the transmitter even working? While Etta James' record *Wall Flower* played, I rushed out and snapped on the radio by Donna's typewriter. The singer was dancing with Henry in the lobby exactly as she was in the control room. I let out a "yahoo" and ran back to the control room. *My voice has been going out into the night, too!*

When the clock hit midnight, I wound up *Frantic 'Lantic*, read the sign-off announcement reminding listeners "We'll be back on the air at 6 a.m." and finished with an enthusiastic "Good-night." Leaning back in the chair, a rush of accomplishment swept through me. *Done! My first time on the air!*

There was one more thing to do. I played the one cut on a shiny black disc labeled "Sign-Off Song," and a chorus began to sing.

"Oh, I wish I was in the land of cotton..."

REALITY OF THE JOB

Exhilarated from my broadcasting debut, I ran down the shell road from the boarding house the next morning. *Maybe there's more to do on the air at the station – finish Carl's shift, or relieve Jerry for three or four hours.*

I burst through the door of the lobby, and Phil Rice looked up from his newspaper.

"'Heard you last night," he said. "Good job." He went back to reading and my chest swelled and my head, too.

John Kenworthy came out of his office rubbing his hands.

"Okay, Davey-boy, now you're going to learn how to do the log."

My jaw dropped. *Introduce songs and spin records is what I want to "do."* I was smart enough not to say anything.

Donna sat in her chair at the typewriter.

"Good morning," she said sweetly.

I grumbled a greeting, pulled the wicker chair over and sat next to her.

"Orders from advertisers are snapped in here," she said as she slid a small two-ring binder to me.

I thumbed through the thin pink pages and saw the names of the salesmen. "Rice" was Phil and "Smith" was

Hamp Smith, the one I hadn't met. A few orders showed "House."

"Who's this guy 'House'?" I asked. Donna laughed.

"Those are the advertisers that Kenworthy handles," she said. "He's management, so he isn't paid a commission. Those accounts are held by 'the house' – y'know, like in Las Vegas." I felt like a jerk, not because I didn't know what "House" meant, but that Donna laughed at me.

"These are the flex line holders," she said pointing to an odd contraption on her desk. Metal frames hooked on a stand reminded me of jukebox titles held in glass bubbles at diners back in Jersey.

"Snap a flex line into one of them," Donna said, handing a strip of yellow cardboard that I fumbled and dropped on her desk. Bending the strip, I jammed it onto a frame. Donna sighed, but continued.

"Advertisers' names are typed on the flex lines. Look at the sales orders for the day you're working on and swap around the lines in the appropriate frames. Understand?"

I grunted that I did, although I didn't.

"Let me get you some blank flex lines for new advertisers." She leaned in front of me to open a drawer and her hair smelled terrific.

"When you finish setting up a day, follow what's on each frame and type a page for each hour." *Type?* I took typing in high school and never got the knack of using all my fingers and thumbs.

Donna rose from her chair, her hip brushing my shoulder.

"I've set up the frames for tomorrow's log," she said. "You go ahead and type."

I sat in the chair still warm from her body. I rolled in a blank log form to the dark red Smith Corona electric typewriter. Squinting at the first frame to find the advertiser's name at the top, I pressed a key. The typewriter sat there.

"You have to turn it on," Donna said as she pulled the wicker chair across the lobby. Feeling underneath the machine, I found a switch, pressed it and the beast began to whir. I started again with the first letter. The typewriter took off and printed it five times before my finger released the key. Embarrassed, I looked over at Donna. She sat down and, with a flash of her leg, picked up a magazine.

Continuing to squint at flex lines as I hunted for letters on the keyboard, I pecked away until Carl came out of the control room.

"How did it go last night, Dave?"

"Great." I didn't tell him how I froze in the chair on wheels.

Jerry Girard came in the front door.

"Everything okay last night?" he said.

"Yep." I didn't mention how I missed transmitter readings all evening and copied his.

"Y'know, I had the weirdest feeling last night," I said. Donna looked up from her magazine. "Like I was in a room talking to myself."

"Oh, people heard you, all right," Carl said.

"When I'm on," Jerry added, "I imagine there's at least one little old lady listening out there." I thought of Mrs. McGarrity, sitting in her rocker on the porch at the boarding house, listening to the plug-in radio on the window sill. I shook that image out of my head. *Maybe I should imagine younger Donna when I'm on next.*

As the hour wore on, my frustration grew with the task of typing. Wanting to shout "Enough," I pulled the last page from the Smith Corona and waved it in the air like a soldier surrendering with a white flag.

"Good," Donna said, and she clapped her hands.

* * *

"Howdy. You must be Dave." A heavy-set man extended a big mitt of a hand. "I'm Hamp Smith." He eased into the chair at his desk and eyed me up and down.

"So, you're another one of them boys sent down here from Neeew York City."

"Yessir," I replied.

"Heard you last night," he said. "Pretty good for a beginner."

"Thank you," I said.

We looked at each other. Hampton Smith, brown from the sun, wearing blue jeans and a t-shirt with words "Gone Fishin'" on the front, and me, a pale skinny kid in chinos and a polo shirt with my high school logo on the breast pocket.

The evening before, I had heard him talk on his recorded show about the best spots for fishing along the Grand Strand. "Man, they were bitin' good today at Murrells Inlet."

Our gaze at each other was broken by the station manager bouncing out of his office.

"Dave, you're going on the air earlier this evening," John Kenworthy said. "Get with Jerry for what you need to know." He rushed to the front door and called over his shoulder. "Carl's going back on his night shift next Monday, and you're going to start doing the morning show." He flew outside and I stood, stunned.

The morning show! More listeners! The big time in Myrtle Beach!

MY BIG ERROR

Anticipation to be a morning star began the moment Kenworthy said I was switching to the wake-up show. I yearned to make the move right away, but it was only Wednesday, and I had to continue working the evening shift the rest of the week. Monday morning seemed a million days away.

Because I had gone on the previous night at eight p.m., Jerry had to tell me what to do on the air for the first two hours of the evening shift starting at six. While he played records on his afternoon show, I sat behind him and listened as he rattled off the instructions. Lacking the good sense to use a pen and notepad, I struggled to absorb everything he said and kept nodding and saying "Uh huh."

"Be sure you read a spot for Chapin's when it's on the log," he said. "And remember to play Hadacol." WMYB's biggest advertiser was a department store in Myrtle Beach owned by the Chapin family. Hadacol was another story.

A large black vinyl disc contained 60-second messages on both sides featuring a pitch man with a thick Southern accent. He called his listeners "friends" and extolled the virtues of the elixir Hadacol he claimed could cure ailments from rheumatism to "the heebie-jeebies."

Through Slanted Windows

"I tried it once." Jerry said. "It's not bad if you mix it with Pepsi."

He finished his instructions, and I went to "the music library" to pull records ahead of time for the upcoming evening stint. Hamp Smith came in the control room and interrupted my fun.

"Here's tonight's *Gone Fishin'*," he said, and handed me a reel of tape. "Make sure you get it on at 6:30." I placed the tape by the control board and went back to the more important task of choosing music.

At six o'clock, Jerry got up from the chair, and I slipped in to take my place between the turntables. His last record ended, and without even looking, my fingers went right to the microphone switch. Attempting to go from tenor to baritone, I introduced the next program and started the first record, "The Great Pretender." *Funny, I'm not nervous like last night. It's all happening naturally.*

Giving the log a glance, I saw a live spot for Chapin's and a recorded one for Hadacol. I pushed the log aside and enjoyed the bliss of being a disc jockey.

At seven o'clock, a red bulb flashed on the wall indicating someone was outside. While Patti Page sang "I Went to Your Wedding," I dashed to the lobby and opened the door. Hamp Smith was there.

"My tape!" he yelled. "You didn't play it at six thirty!" His brown face had turned red. "I had a potential sponsor listening." His wife stood behind him, a frown on her face, and said nothing. Carried away with playing records, I hadn't looked far enough down the log page and failed to put his program on the air.

"I'm s-sorry," I stammered.

"Dammit," he said, and stomped down the gravel path to his car.

Back in the control room, my hands shook and my stomach churned. I feared my voice would choke with shame when I went back on the air. I didn't want to open the microphone, but I swallowed the lump in my throat and reached for the switch.

The shaking subsided by the time the program of dance music started. Mixing Artie Shaw and Benny Goodman into the swinging sounds of Count Basie eased the turmoil in my stomach. I scoured the remaining pages of the log, so I wouldn't miss anything else. Like a dope, I turned back to the six o'clock page, and there it was, *Gone Fishin'* at six-thirty. The image of Hamp Smith at the door made my stomach flip again.

Before the eleven o'clock news, I propped the control room door open with the trash can and checked the teletype machine. *How awful if the lobby is filled with Kenworthy, Donna and my radio buddies scolding me and shaking their fingers.*

Switching from disc jockey to newsman, I settled down and tried to sound like Edward R. Murrow. One of the stories was about a bus accident in Boca Raton, Florida. I'd heard of rattan furniture and knew it was popular in tropical climates, so I pronounced the name of the town "Boca Rattan."

As soon as I kicked off *Frantic 'Lantic Beach Party* with Muddy Waters' "Still a Fool," the white light on the tan cradle phone flashed. A man was on the line.

"I've traveled the country – no, the world – and the name of that town in your news is pronounced 'Boca Ra-tone'," he said and hung up.

Golly, someone was listening.

* * *

The next morning, I hunched over the Smith Corona and stole a look around the lobby. Donna sat in the wicker chair, her eyes glued to a magazine. Phil Rice shuffled the newspaper, cleared his throat and didn't say a word. Hamp Smith was at his desk with his chair turned back to me. The room was deathly quiet except for my pecks on the typewriter.

John Kenworthy came bustling through the front door and rushed to his office. I'm sure Smith had told him of my foul-up the night before. The manager's voice was muffled as he talked on the phone until he yelled loud and clear.

"Dave, come in here a minute."

Oh, Lord, two days in radio, and I'm being fired. Terrified, I stumbled into his office. Holding my breath, I stood rigid in front of Kenworthy's desk.

"I need you to stay awhile after sign-off tonight," he said. "Our contract engineer is coming up from Charleston to do a frequency check, and he needs your help. His name's Redmond."

My shoulders slumped in relief, and I took a breath.

"Okay," I croaked.

As I left his office, Kenworthy called after me.

"Keep your eye on the ball, son."

Back at the typewriter, I sat for a moment. *Have I learned anything from last night? I guess responsibility comes with having fun in radio.*

* * *

I didn't want to go on the air that evening, Thursday. Pushing the control room door open an inch, I peeked at Jerry.

"C'mon in, Dave, I'm not staying here 'til midnight."

As I entered, the room felt cold. The album covers on the record shelves were dull and had no enticement. The control board had turned back into the four-foot monster.

When Jerry got up from the chair at six o'clock, I hesitated before moving in. *No one else is going to keep the station going. I'm it.*

First things first. I bent over and with shaking fingers threaded the reel on the tape machine for *Gone Fishin'.* I felt relieved I handled it before anything else, but then the picture of Hamp Smith at the door the previous night popped in my head, and my stomach churned. Sitting down, I grabbed a pen and underlined every commercial on the log for Chapin's and Hadacol. Titles for programs on the network were in capital letters, but I underscored them with blue slashes. Finally, I was able to stand at "the music library" for the more pleasant task of selecting records.

Later in the evening, it was comforting to hear the familiar "dum-de-dum-dum" of *Dragnet* from NBC at nine o'clock. Lying in bed as a kid, I had listened to the cop show, the only light in the room coming from the radio above my pillow. *Now here I am, working at a radio station and sending Dragnet into the night sky.*

Before midnight, the red bulb for the front door flashed. Making sure there was enough time left on The Drifters' "Ruby Baby," I went to the lobby. Standing under the light outside was a tall, thin man in blue jeans and denim jacket. He yelled his name and I opened the door then hopped aside so he wouldn't smack my leg with the metal tool chest he lugged in. Brushing past me, the man went straight to the control room. The engineer from Charleston had arrived.

Placing the chest by the transmitter, Redmond knelt on one knee and snapped open its twin lids. Trays popped up with a jumble of pliers, screw drivers, twisted wire and a squashed coil of solder. I thought of my father's tools hanging neatly in a row back home.

"Go ahead and give your regular sign-off, but don't turn off the transmitter," he said. "Play some music and keep giving call letters and location every twenty seconds." I looked at him with a quizzical expression. "A monitoring station up on Long Island will be listening to see if we've drifted off frequency." *Oh.*

At midnight, I started an album by the swinging big band of Neal Hefti. Redmond stood by the cradle phone waiting for a call from Long Island. His instructions about "giving call letters and location every twenty seconds" sounded like an April Fool's day joke, but I kept watching the clock and opening the microphone at the appropriate time.

"This is WMYB, Myrtle Beach, South Carolina."

I imagined engineers zeroing in on my voice with their sophisticated equipment from a thousand miles away. As I continued to speak, it dawned on me. *I'm being heard in New York!*

"Can I give my name?" I asked Redmond.

"Don't be smart," he said.

* * *

The next evening, Friday, was much better. With renewed confidence, I swaggered into the station like an old pro. As Jerry went out the front door, I remained standing in the control room and surveyed my surroundings.

Light streaming in the back window from the setting sun added to the soft glow of the overhead fluorescent. Colorful albums lay on the music shelves waiting for my touch.

The meter on the control board shone like a beacon, lighting the way to the knobs and switches that would let me speak to listeners waiting for my dulcet tones. I sat in the chair and its arms wrapped around me.

Again, I threaded the *Gone Fishin'* reel on the tape before doing anything else. Hamp Smith's program went on promptly at six-thirty. While he talked of the best places to fish, I selected records for the shift.

"How High the Moon" by Les Paul and Mary Ford was a favorite of mine, so I chose to play it for a third night in a row. I remembered how Fred Darwin at the broadcasting school made our class laugh by using a funny line to point out the absurdity of a disc jockey who allows his personal taste to influence his choice of music.

"I'll be playing my favorite songs, and I hope I'll be playing some of yours."

Of course, in no way did that apply to me. I was the exception to the rule as I blissfully picked The Four Freshmen's "Day By Day."

During the dance band show later, the red bulb flashed for the front door. John Kenworthy was outside with his arm around a short, muscular man with crew cut hair.

"Dave, meet Mickey Spillane," he said.

The man gripped my hand with fingers of steel.

Mickey Spillane! He was the author of tough-guy novels filled with exploding guns and hot sex. A copy of his steamy *I, The Jury* had been passed around between boys and girls in my senior year at high school.

"I ran into Mickey at Aunt Belle's Restaurant," Kenworthy said. "He lives down in Murrells Inlet and I wanted to show him the station."

"Hey, kid," Spillane said, stepping in. "Nice place ya got here."

I gawked at him. Working for ABC, I'd bumped into celebrities, but this was different. *A famous person actually shook my hand and spoke to me.* Meeting him got me so wound up, I sailed through *Frantic 'Lantic Beach Party* with an extra shot of adrenaline.

Before turning off the transmitter at midnight, I played the sign-off song, and the chorus began to sing "Dixie." As I scurried around the control room putting away records, the white bulb flashed on the phone. *Another call from a listener?*

A man identified himself as a captain at the Air Force base south of Myrtle Beach.

I'd watched fighter jets scream low over the boardinghouse, and Mrs. McGarrity told me they came from a runway on the edge of the ocean.

"I've fought in two wars and have seen men die for this country," the military man said. "Why don't you play 'The

Star Spangled Banner' when you sign off?" I didn't know how to answer him. Stations in the North played the national anthem when shutting down at night, but being a young man wrapped up in radio, I hadn't given a thought to why we played *Dixie* on WMYB in South Carolina. I mumbled something about calling our manager in the morning. The man hung up.

* * *

After locking the front door, I gazed at the stars and moon – and my stomach growled. Going on the air at six the last three evenings, I had missed the home-cooked meals at Mrs. McGarrity's. Snacks from the vending machine in the lobby didn't stick to my ribs. Besides, when I washed down crackers with Pepsi, the soda tightened my vocal cords and made it difficult to sound like the announcers on NBC.

As I walked up to Ocean Highway and my bed waiting at the boarding house, the smell of cooked meat lured me over to a sandy field. Bare light bulbs strung between live oaks bounced gently in the night breeze. Below, the front window of a clapboard shack was wide open and inviting. The aroma of hamburgers beckoned for me to sit at one of the wooden picnic tables scattered around the field.

A heavy-set woman stood inside the shack scraping grease off a griddle. She saw me and called out "Samantha! Customer!"

A girl my age appeared, wearing a frilly apron on her narrow waist. I watched her shapely legs move in tight blue jeans as she walked towards me, her white t-shirt showing abundant curves. She took a pencil from behind her ear.

"May I help you?" she said, her voice soft with a trace of a southern accent.

"I'd like a hamburger."

"Do you want everything on it?"

"Yes, please." *Oh, God, I sound like a kid at home with his mother.*

She scribbled on a notepad and turned to the shack. My mind flashed on the signs I saw riding in from Florence: "Dr. Pepper 10-2-4." Jerry had told me it was a soda.

"And I'll have a Dr. Pepper," I called after her. She wiggled her pencil in the air to signify she heard me. Watching her hips move as she walked away was a delight. I fiddled with the metal napkin dispenser on the table and pretended to read the plastic covered menu underneath. *Should I try to talk to the girl when she comes back?*

When she returned, I was more taken with the hamburger than with her. Sizzling meat hung over the edge of the flat bottom bun. A pale green lettuce leaf and the white rim of an onion peeked out from the puffy tan bun on top. A slice of wet pickle snuggled against the burger, one end stuck in a heap of hot French fries.

"Mustard and ketchup are there on the table," the girl said, placing a bottle of Dr. Pepper in front of me. "Is there anything else I can get you?"

"No thanks."

She walked to a far table and sat.

Damn it! Why didn't I invite her to sit with me and talk? She's not busy. I'm her only customer. Easy questions I could have asked tumbled in my brain. *Do you live around here? Is that your mom in the shack? Did you see me come out of WMYB? I'm an announcer there, y'know.*

I ate my hamburger in silence while katydids serenaded the night in the swamp grass behind the radio station. *What a jerk I am.*

MORNING GLORY

I hit the pillow at ten o'clock Sunday night and stared at the ceiling. Listening to the ticking of the wind-up clock by the bed and the booming of the surf beyond the dune, my mind kept thinking of what the morning would bring. *This is like the night before Christmas when I was a kid.*

The alarm was set to go off at 4:30 a.m. *That should give me plenty of time to shower, get dressed and be over to the station by five.* A full hour in the control room is what I needed to be fully prepared before going on the air with my dawn debut. I looked at the clock. Ten-thirty. *This is stupid.*

I swung my legs off the bed, snapped on the wall lamp and reached for the *Collier's* magazine pilfered from Mrs. McGarritty's sitting room. Lying back in the dim light, I began to read. My eyes closed after the first article.

When the alarm rang, I reached over quickly and slapped the button on the clock to stop it. *I hope Jerry didn't hear it on the other side of the bathroom.* Using a drizzle of water, I showered quietly, then dressed in clothes put aside in the closet the night before, careful the wire hangers didn't jangle against each other and wake the other boarders.

I tiptoed along the hall and down the stairs, every other step creaking on the warped wood. The hinges on the wobbly screen door of the porch squeaked as I eased it closed so the spring wouldn't make it bang. My shoes crunched with every footfall on the shell road.

Waiting until a milk truck sped by, I crossed Ocean Highway. An empty blue and white patrol car was parked a block away at the Streamline Diner. *The officer must be inside having coffee. It's good to know someone else is awake.* Passing the hamburger shack, I thought of the girl with the curves in her blue jeans. *Is she somewhere in bed, her legs curled up, asleep?*

Stumbling in the dark on the gravel path outside WMYB, I took the station key from my wallet. *What if I drop it in the weeds? I'll be on my hands and knees hunting for it for an hour.* My fingers searched for the lock on the front door, and when I found it, I tapped with the tip of the key to find the slot. *I bet Rayburn and Finch don't have to do this every morning at WNEW.*

I believed that when I opened the door, an exciting new world of radio would be blossoming forth with the golden opportunity for me to be a stellar morning personality and entertain listeners eager to hear me.

The lobby was pitch black.

Stepping in, I shuffled sideways, feeling my way along the front wall until I came to a light switch. I snapped it up, and the lobby became as bright as my parent's living room on Christmas morning.

The fluorescent light in the control room ceiling flashed when I turned it on, and I blinked. My eyes went from the desk and the turntables to the records on the shelves to the transmitter silent and foreboding at the back wall. The feeling of intimidation grabbed hold again. *This is like the first time I set foot in here.* My mind raced over the list of instructions from Carl and began to put everything in sequence for the sign-on shift. I hitched up my pants and got to work.

Beginning at the desk, I turned on power to the turntables, but ignored the switch to the control board. Juice was already running to it. The metal top was warm to my touch, the meter behind the glass on the front glowed yellow, and the needle inside lay at rest, ready to jump up with the first sound of my voice. I remembered the note Carl made sure I read the first day in the control room. It was printed in bold letters and stapled to the cork board by the engineer from Charleston.

"The control board stays ON always!!! Don't turn it off – ever!!! The pre-amps won't come back on if you do. Redmond."

To ensure there'd be news to deliver at six o'clock, I ran to the lobby and flipped the switch on the teletype. The machine came to life and began to hammer out reports of what had happened in the world while people slept in Myrtle Beach.

Rushing back to the control room, I went to the "the music library" and shuffled through the 45 records in green sleeves. John Kenworthy's edict on Friday resounded in my head.

"No sultry ballads Monday morning. Plenty of up-tempo stuff. Guy Mitchell, Theresa Brewer. Happy songs are all I wanna hear."

Finally, I was able to listen to the special radio Carl showed me behind the transmitter. The snap of a knob brought in the voice from Colorado.

"Naval Observatory Master Clock. At the tone, three hours, twelve minutes, and thirty-five seconds, Mountain Daylight Time." When a beep sounded, I looked around at our clock and added two hours for Eastern Time. The announcer in Colorado continued to give the time every five seconds until I turned him off. *What a boring job that must be.*

As I worked, I broke up the early morning congestion in my vocal cords by singing the scale. "Do re mi fa so la ti do." Remembering the exercise at the broadcasting school to loosen facial muscles, I stretched my lips and said the vowels of the alphabet out loud with great exaggeration. "A E I O U." I repeated them three times until my face hurt. Bending over, I touched my toes, one, two, three times. Straightening up, I held both arms out and twisted my torso from right to left, one, two, three times.

Then I stepped lively again to the teletype machine in the lobby, ripped off a sheet of paper and dragged it to the control room. It snagged at the door, but I gave it a stiff yank and it followed me in. Glancing at the clock above the control board, I panicked and dropped the sheet on the desk. *Where did the hour go? It's time to fire up the transmitter!*

I faced the six-foot hulk of steel in back of the room. With three meters along the top, the thick glass window on the front and two red buttons staring like large eyes, the transmitter looked like a crazy robot from a science fiction movie. *What order do I push the buttons?* Jerry had told me how to turn off the thing at midnight with "Right button first then the left." Carl's voice echoed in my brain to turn it on, "Left one first, then the right." *That makes sense.* I pushed them in the correct order and stepped back, afraid there'd be an explosion, but the needles in the meters woke up, stood at attention and the transmitter began to hum. Delighted with the accomplishment, I turned around too quick and my feet tangled. I tripped and caught myself on the big turntable cabinet at the end of the desk. *I can't slow down. I've got to prepare a newscast.*

As the clock's hands raced to six a.m., I tore out a summary of news from the teletype paper with my hands. *I'll find the ruler later.* With no time to read over the reports, I decided to deliver the newscast "cold." *What if there are difficult names to trip me? Oh, well, who's listening this early anyway?* I signed on the station and started my morning debut as a newsman.

My eyes looked ahead at the words on the ragged piece of paper before my mouth said them, a trick I learned at the broadcasting school. The news was written plain and simple with nothing odd to pronounce, except when coming to the riots in Hungary. I stopped for a second and looked at the name of political figure Imre Nagy. *Im-ree Na-gee? Im-ra Naggy?* I chose to say "Im-ree Na-gee." After agonizing with a vain attempt to sound like Edward R. Murrow, I threw the paper on the floor and started a turntable. Eddie Fisher began to sing "Dungaree Doll," and I became the more relaxed host of the wake-up show.

It didn't take long to realize it was busier than the evening shift. Although I'd typed the log the previous Friday, I had forgotten there were more advertisers scheduled in the morning than an occasional Chapin's or Hadacol.

I read commercials from the copy book, plowing through thirty and sixty-second messages and ten-second "shorties." It was a struggle to get all the spots on the air between records. Trying to sound chipper as I announced, I couldn't lose the "I-just- woke-up" roughness in my voice.

To add a variety to my selection of singers, I followed Eddie Fisher's record with one by Kay Starr and then one from The Four Aces. As the hour went on, my idea of "first male-then female-then group" fell apart. If a song ran out before I had another one set up, I grabbed any record I could lay my hands on, slapped it on a turntable and put the needle down, hoping it would be on the first groove.

Sheets of teletype paper built up around my feet as I searched for scores of major league baseball games. It was hard to choose which ones to announce. *Are the listeners in Myrtle Beach really interested in the New York Yankees?* I decided to give scores for all the teams.

Kenworthy told me Friday that listeners wanted to know how cool or warm the air is in the morning, so I rose from the desk every fifteen minutes to check the temperature out the back window. The sun lit the swamp grass brighter every time I squinted at the number by the red liquid in the thermometer.

Remembering the law dictated by the Federal Communications Commission, I went back to the transmitter every thirty minutes and read the numbers the needles pointed to. *God forbid we're exceeding our power of one-thousand watts and my voice is spreading out all over South Carolina.* I scribbled the numbers as fast as I could in the printed form on the clipboard.

Fearing something new may have happened in the world since I last checked the teletype, I ran to the machine three times each hour. No ocean liner sinking or typhoon occurred, but fresh summaries of news were waiting on the ream of paper that continued to spew from the top. Back in the control room, I rehearsed the reports out loud while records played, and at seven and eight o'clock, became a newsman again.

By nine o'clock, I was exhausted. Slumping in the chair, I let my arms hang loose. Georgia Gibbs sang "Tweedle Dee," but my foot didn't tap.

Station people arrived to begin their day. Kenworthy stuck his head in the control room.

"Everything alright, kid?"

Donna entered and stood by my chair.

"I heard you this morning," she said in her sweet voice.

Phil Rice came in to use the bathroom and didn't say a word.

The preacher from the local Pentecostal church showed up at nine for his daily fifteen-minute broadcast. It didn't require me to do anything, just turn on the microphone in the studio next door and let him rip. Thankful for the break, I staggered to the lobby for a package of Oreos from the snack machine. *Not a fitting breakfast for a morning radio personality. I'll bet John Gambling at WOR has a caterer.*

When the preacher finished, I played a bunch of popular records, but couldn't muster the energy to do much talking between them. Bert Parks rescued me at ten o'clock with his *Bandstand* program from NBC.

* * *

Before going to the station the next morning at dawn, I ate breakfast at the Streamline Diner. Perched on a round seat at the counter, I slurped a runny fried egg and poked at white lumps called "grits." *What if this makes me burp on the air?* I pushed the plate away and took a swallow of watery orange juice.

The second day of the wake-up show was not as frantic as the first. I established a routine where I jumped up from the desk only once in the hour to check the teletype, transmitter and thermometer together. It was still hard to get all the commercials on the air. The six o'clock hour wasn't as jammed as seven and eight, so I looked ahead at the next two pages of the log, stole spots from those hours, and put them on earlier.

Before nine o'clock, John Kenworthy stopped in the control room. As Don Cherry sang "It Isn't Fair," I complained about the abundance of commercials in the three hours.

"It's hard to cram them all in."

The station manager proceeded to teach me how to do a "double spot."

"After a record, read a spot, then say 'the time is' or give the weather or a score while you turn the page in the copy book. Read the next spot and play another song. Keep up that pattern and you'll get 'em all in." A bulb went on in my head, and the business of broadcasting became easier for me right then.

HALF THE DREAM

Every morning after finishing the wake-up show, I opened the door of the control room, and rested my back against the frame. I'd take a deep breath, but seeing the Smith Corona in the lobby, I would slump. *Oh, no. I have to type tomorrow's log.*

I regarded the traffic job as a dreaded task. An eighteen-page log of commercials had to be typed daily for the following day, and a total of three had to be produced on Friday for the weekend and Monday. Besides seven logs a week, the copy book in the control room had to be kept current and that was my job, too. I pulled outdated commercials from the three-ring binder and filed them alphabetically in a four-drawer cabinet next to my desk. If a new piece of copy handed to me by a salesman was scheduled more than once a day, I had to sit at the Smith Corona and type the words on a stencil.

Clamping the stencil on the drum of a Ditto machine, I cranked the handle and churned out the number of copies needed. As they slid into a tray, the duplicating fluid on the wet shiny paper had a sour smell. So did the traffic job. *I'm not an announcer. I'm a damn typist, file clerk and Ditto operator.*

*   *   *

"You boys aren't smoking out there, are you?"

Mrs. McGarrity peered through the lace curtains of an open window.

"No, ma'am," I replied.

Jerry Girard, Carl Grand and I lounged on the porch of the boarding house. Two part-time announcers came up from the air base each Sunday to keep the station running, so the three of us full-timers had the whole day off to relax and shoot the breeze.

We swapped stories of how we got to Myrtle Beach. Both Jerry and Carl received their training at the prestigious Columbia School of Broadcasting in Manhattan.

"Does the school really have a lot of classrooms?" I asked Jerry.

"Yeah. I got lost in the hall my first night."

"You wouldn't believe Broadcast Coaching Associates," I said. "Three guys taught us in a rehearsal hall for dancers, and the control room was a little bigger than a closet." They laughed.

We discovered the three of us had been sent by instructors to be interviewed by Olin Tice, the announcer at CBS and owner of WMYB.

"One of my teachers is a news director with an odd name at ABC," Jerry said.

"Telly Savalas, right? You run into him at ABC, Dave?" Carl asked.

I shook my head. "Nope."

"Anyway," Jerry continued, "he set up a meeting for me with Tice. Savalas said I'd be a jerk not to take the job in Myrtle Beach. 'Geez, the beach and all,' he said. Olin Tice has other stations in Lake City and Moncks Corner, too, you know."

Carl and I nodded.

"I was sent to meet Tice by one of my teachers at BCA with another odd name – Ernie Althschuler," I said. "He's an engineer at CBS and works with Tice on a program. He told me Tice likes to hire guys like us in New York and send them down here because he thinks our Yankee accents lend sophistication to his stations." I held up my hand with thumb and forefinger together and pretended to take a dainty sip from an imaginary tea cup. We all laughed.

Jerry Girard went on to say he was raised on the mean streets of the Bronx. Carl Grand said he was from the rundown factory town of Bridgeport, Connecticut. Their eyes grew wide when I described Ridgewood, New Jersey. "It's pretty snooty," I said. "There're no hotels to attract 'intruders' and Jewish store owners can't live in the town and have to leave by sundown."

We were silent for a moment while a motorcycle roared up the highway.

"Girard is actually my first name," Jerry said. "My last name's really Suglia. I think Girard Suglia sounds too Italian."

"I'm keeping Archard," I said, "Although some think it's 'Archer'."

"My last name is just 'Grand' with me," Carl said.

Jerry and I groaned.

Carl took a swallow from a bottle of Dr. Pepper.

"I'm glad I'm back on the evening shift," he said. "I like sleeping 'til noon then hitting the beach in the afternoon."

Jerry shifted in a canvas beach chair.

"Kenworthy's driving to Charlotte on a sales trip again this week. When he gets back, he'll have a trunk full of albums from record distributors." *I hope there'll an LP by the Hi-Los.*

"My voice is thick when I go on in the morning," I said.

"Try drinking grapefruit juice," Jerry suggested.

He put down his Pepsi.

Through Slanted Windows

"I can't wait until football begins at the high school. I convinced Kenworthy we should broadcast their games. Sports – that's what I want to do."

Carl put his arms behind his head.

"I'd like to own a radio station some day. Maybe out west. Yeah, California."

My confession came next.

"I want to be on WNEW in New York."

Jerry let out a low whistle, and Carl moved his hand palm down indicating "smooth." We stopped talking and listened to the booming of the surf beyond the dune.

I didn't tell my radio buddies then how frustrated I was performing the traffic duties at WMYB and how I wished I could be on the air eight hours a day.

* * *

As the weeks went by, I dutifully tackled the job of typing logs and keeping the copy book up-to-date, and kept my mouth shut and didn't complain. At least I was living half my dream each day by being an entertainer on the air in the control room before becoming a slave to the Smith Corona in the lobby.

At the end of summer, I did my first remote broadcast. Carl and I stood in the garden department of Chapin's and told listeners of the big discounts on spades, hoes and wheel barrows.

The first Friday night in September, I was perched with Jerry on the top row of the bleachers at Myrtle Beach High. He held a small console on his lap with one hand and gripped a microphone with the other as he described the school's football game. Sitting next to him, I did my best to jot down on a clipboard the numbers of first downs and yards gained as the wind kept blowing the paper.

Every time when I pulled the last page of a log from the typewriter at the station, I fantasized about being a DJ at

WNEW. I pictured myself spinning records in a maroon and grey studio like Jazzbo, with an engineer bouncing in his chair to the beat of the music.

On the porch Sundays with Jerry and Carl, I thought about what I really wanted to do in radio and how to achieve it. Obviously, if I wanted something more than what the station in Myrtle Beach offered, I'd have to move on. An idea hatched in the back of my brain. *Wheels! I need a car.*

* * *

While the preacher was on the air one morning, I went to the lobby. Phil Rice sat at his desk reading the Charleston newspaper.

"Mr. Rice, Eddie's Auto Mart is your account, right?"

Without looking up, he replied. "Yep."

"Do you suppose you can get me a deal on a car?"

"When I get off after the news, we'll go see."

Riding in Mr. Rice's four-door Chrysler, I saw more of Myrtle Beach than the boarding house and diner around the station. We passed the long gray building of Chapin's Department Store and I got my first look at WMYB's biggest advertiser. Mannequins wearing sweaters stood rigid with pumpkins at their feet.

"I have to stop there later and pick up a new ad," Mr. Rice muttered. *Oh, great. Something else for me to put in the copy book.*

Eddie's Auto Mart was a block beyond. Used cars were displayed in rows with words scrawled in white shoe polish on the windows: "Clean," "Sharp," "Low Miles." Tattered pennants flapped overhead, and a banner with a misspelled word billowed like a sail between light poles: "Big Bargins." Mr. Rice parked on the weed-covered lot in front of a plywood shack.

The owner approached, a pudgy man wearing a checkered sport coat held by a button straining at his middle.

"Phil, ya bastard, who's the kid?" Eddie yelled.

"Dave from the radio station," Mr. Rice said. "He wants a car."

Eddie shook my hand and eyed me up and down, figuring how much cash I had.

"Look 'em over, son. I'm in a generous mood today."

Mr. Rice and Eddie jawboned at the shack, and I walked along a line of cars. They stuck their hoods out at me like puppies in a pet store: A pale green hot rod sported red flames on the doors, its back end jacked up on over-sized bald tires; a gangster-type black sedan sat low and frowned under a metal visor across the windshield; a creamy white convertible had its blond top pulled back exposing cracked leather seats. All the cars had scratches and dents on their bodies.

"How much for this blue Frazer on the end?" I shouted.

"Ah, a man with elegant taste," Eddie said as he hustled over. "You can have it for seventy-five bucks." I had paid forty-five for the '41 Plymouth in Jersey two years ago, but the car on Eddie's lot wasn't as old and there were no tears in the upholstery.

"All I can afford is sixty," I said, hoping my fib wouldn't turn my face red.

The man took the stub of a cigar from his mouth "We'll talk. Go ahead, take her for a spin."

Eddie tossed me the keys and I scrambled behind the wheel of the Frazer. Starting the engine, I was surprised to hear a pleasant purr. The gas and brake pedals were worn despite the scant miles in the odometer on the dashboard. *But hey, there's no clutch. The car's got automatic drive!*

Tooling up *Ocean Highway*, I recalled reading in Dad's *Automotive News* how a Mr. Kaiser and a Mr. Frazer built stylish cars after World War II that turned the auto industry on its ear. I was elated to be driving one of them. Turning the car onto the highway to Florence, I let out a "yahoo" and sped out to the countryside.

Eddie's voice echoed in my head – "We'll talk" –and my stomach churned. *That means we have to dicker about the price. How am I going to do that?*

I pulled the car off the road and parked under the comfort of a spreading oak.

Putting my forehead on the steering wheel, I refigured my budget. After paying for room and dinners at Mrs. McGarrity's, laundry, breakfast at the diner and daily candy bars from the vending machine at the station, I had a small amount of cash left over each week. *But then there'll be gas for the Frazer and oil every thousand miles.* I looked at the frightened face in the rear view mirror. *What if I can't get Eddie to come down? Should I fudge and tell him the transmission is noisy or the brakes are mushy?* Wiping my sweaty hands on my chinos, I turned the Frazer around and headed back to the Auto Mart. *I can do this.*

Driving up to Eddie and Mr. Rice, I rolled down the window and began.

"Sixty dollars!"

"Seventy two fifty," Eddie shot back.

The wallet in my hip pocket seemed to go flatter.

"Sixty three," I countered.

"Geez, Louise, I gotta pay the rent," the used car magnate said. "I need seventy."

I pictured dollar bills with wings flapping away in my mind.

"Sixty four fifty." I tried to make my voice sound as firm as I could.

Eddie squinted at me. "I like your moxie, kid, although Rice here is a horse's ass. I like all you guys at WMY and B, so tell ya what – gimme sixty eight bucks and the car's yours."

My heart jumped. "Okay!" *There go eggs in the morning and candy bars for awhile, but now I have car.*

Mr. Rice watched solemnly as I signed papers in the office. Eddie handed me the title and keys adding in a low voice, "That's one of the first Frazer's off the line in forty-six, son. Treat her good."

I shook his hand and thanked Phil Rice for driving me to Eddie's.

"I'll beat you back to the station," I said and ran to the car.

Starting it up, I tromped on the gas pedal and the rear wheels spit stones as the car tore out of the lot. I angled the side vent window to let air blow in and my mind raced with the engine. *Why, this car can take me to wherever there's a bigger and better job in radio.*

* * *

After John Kenworthy read his copy of *Broadcasting-Telecasting* each week, he'd toss it on the end table in the lobby. Picking up the magazine one morning, I perused the *Help Wanted – Announcers* column on a back page. One of the ads wanted an announcer to handle on-air duties at WLDB in Atlantic City, New Jersey. It didn't mention typing, filing and duplicating, and no address was given for mailing a tape and resume, only a man's name and telephone number. *Whoever he is, he must be desperate and needs someone right away.*

I looked around at empty WMYB. Donna had left for the university in Columbia, Rice, Smith and Kenworthy were out selling air-time, and Jerry wouldn't be in until noon. Closing the door to the control room, I reached for the phone.

The man in the ad turned out to be the owner of WLDB. After we talked, he had me read something for him over the phone. Clutching the receiver like a field reporter would hold a microphone to describe a disaster, I put the mouthpiece by my lips and delivered a spot for Chapin's department store from the copy book. When I finished, the man on the other end of the line hired me.

In September of 1956, I worked out the two-week notice I gave John Kenworthy, and said good-bye to Jerry, Carl, Phil Rice and even Hamp Smith. Before I left, I thought it would be smart to record an "air check" of myself doing the wake-up show. When I packed at the boarding house, I put that reel of tape in my suit case.

Making sure Mrs. McGarrity was paid up for room and board, I told her how another job had opened, and that I was leaving. The woman looked sad as she placed her hand on my arm. "You're such a nice young man," she said.

I drove the Frazer down the shell road, took a last look at the radio station across *Ocean Highway*, then turned the car and headed north.

CODA

In spite of my high hopes, the job at WLDB in Atlantic City wasn't what I wanted. Programming was a conglomeration of everything the Mutual network sent down the line interspersed with local blocks of recorded music. I had to play marching bands, polka bands, even selections by a schmaltzy orchestra led by a "waltz king." The station was owned and operated by the man I auditioned for on the phone and his wife. He'd come in the control room and tell me to do something on the air *his* way then she'd come in later and tell me to do it *her* way. After three months there, I gave notice. By Christmas, I was back at my father's house, unemployed and licking my wounds.

I didn't believe it then, but in January 1957 a benevolent force nudged me to answer an ad in *Broadcasting-Telecasting* magazine. After sending my resume and the air check tape, I was hired as an announcer at WPME in Punxsutawney, Pennsylvania. It was there I met a girl named Pat and by August, we were married. Early the next year, I landed a job with a station in Tampa, Florida, and Pat was expecting our first child.

As WALT's fast-talking morning man, I was the first DJ to introduce the zip- bang Top Forty format to the west coast of Florida. Listeners woke up to an eclectic mix of singers like black rocker Fats Domino followed by teen idol Frankie Avalon then country crooner Jim Reeves. Their records were among forty listed together in the Top Sellers chart of weekly *Billboard* magazine.

Four years later, I shed the mantle of "disc jockey" and made a serious move to Miami, Florida with Pat and our family that had grown to three children. At WFUN, I wrote advertising copy and won an industry ADDY award for my work. After watching my creative endeavors enable the sales staff to reap rewards in handsome commissions, I realized my next logical step was to become an account executive, too. When my kids asked what I did for a living, I told them "I sell time."

The sales manager at WFUN left to join "a young, dynamic broadcasting company" in the soybean fields of central Illinois, and he convinced me to follow him. I endured "selling time" for WDZ, Decatur in the blowing snow, driving sleet and glazing ice of two winters until Pat and our family of now five yearned to return to the Sunshine State. I did, too.

In 1969, I was rescued by the owner of a three-station chain in Florida who hired me to be sales manager at WMFJ, Daytona Beach. When FM radio burst upon the scene, I moved across town to manage sales and operations for Love 94.5. Because the format was reminiscent of easy-listening WPAT decades ago, the station rose to unbelievable heights in Arbitron audience surveys. Selling time was easy for me as advertisers were eager to have their messages aired on an adult-oriented station situated among a bevy of rock 'n' roll outlets.

How funny it is when I recall the traffic job at WMYB. Although I disliked it at the time, working with salesmen and typing the log was the best lesson I learned in the business – that radio *is* a business. Like other DJs – some of us, admittedly, the prima donnas of the radio world – I once regarded commercials as interruptions to the legitimacy of our art. However, I discovered early in my career that revenue from advertisers is how a radio station pays its electric bill and, more importantly, its announcers.

I never became an air personality at WNEW in New York City. Still, when Pat and I flew to Newark Airport to attend my first high school reunion, I jumped in the rental car and quickly tuned the radio to 1130. Driving up the Garden State Parkway to Ridgewood, we listened to Jonathon Schwartz play one Sinatra song after another.

I didn't make it to any other station in the Mecca of Broadcasting. I found there were better, more stable things in life than the uncertain glamour of the big time – a loving wife, the joy of children, the satisfaction of being a large broadcast fish in a small-market pond.

Retired now, I search the dial when traveling to catch a signal that might be sending out Ella or Frank or the Four Freshmen, but alas, it's a futile attempt. When occasionally visiting radio stations, I feel I'm on the outside looking in as I did as a kid. I wonder if I could work in the business as it is today. The technology of satellite-delivered programming is intriguing, but music for most stations is selected by computers from thousands of miles away. I'd much rather pull a platter from a shiny album cover, cue it on a turntable and chat about the piece of music before letting it spin.

My own dreams and my place in the industry changed over time, but I was fortunate to achieve what I wanted to be from my boyhood – a radio man.